HELP!
My Dog is Scared Of
Fireworks

Toni Shelbourne
&
Karen Bush

Other books by the authors:
HELP! My Dog Doesn't Travel Well in the Car
Toni Shelbourne and Karen Bush

HELP! My Dog is Destroying the Garden
Toni Shelbourne and Karen Bush

HELP! My Dog has a Canine Compulsive Disorder
Toni Shelbourne

The Truth about Wolves and Dogs
Toni Shelbourne *(Hubble & Hattie)*

Among the Wolves: Memoirs of a Wolf Handler
Toni Shelbourne *(Hubble & Hattie)*

Dog-friendly Gardening
Karen Bush *(Hubble & Hattie)*

The Dog Expert
Karen Bush *(Transworld)*

ISBN: 1724559486
ISBN-13: 978-1724559487

ACKNOWLEDGMENTS

We are hugely grateful to all those who offered suggestions, and so generously shared their time and knowledge. We have done our best to ensure that the information contained within is, as far as we can ascertain, correct at time of writing: if there are any errors, then the fault is entirely ours, and not that of those who so kindly put up with our many queries! Among those we would like to thank are:

Sarah Fisher, Robyn Hood, Bob Atkins,
Rachel Jackson, Pete Sherman, Jon Langley,
Tina Constance, Kate Hanley at f+w media,
Amy Snow, Tallgrass Animal Acupressure Institute,
David & Charles

Disclaimer

**For simplicity, throughout this book, dogs of both sexes
are referred to as 'he'**

CONTENTS

vi

1
INTRODUCTION

It's a cold autumn evening: the curtains are drawn, the volume on the television is turned up loud and you've just turned down another social engagement. Sound familiar? If so, then it's probably because you own a dog who is scared of fireworks.

From first-hand experience, we know only too well ourselves just how terrifying the noise of fireworks being let off in your neighbourhood can be for your dog. While you may do your best to calm and comfort your pet, if your best efforts to reassure him don't work you can be left feeling upset at witnessing his distress, and frustrated at being so powerless to help him.

If it were only for a few days during the year you and your dog might be able to live with it, but nowadays, those times of celebration such as Guy Fawkes Night, Independence Day, Thanksgiving Day and Diwali when fireworks are traditionally let off are no longer 'one off' occasions.

Instead they have developed into an entire season, often with so many bangs and whizzes occurring during the weeks before and after the day itself, that it can leave your dog a nervous quivering wreck, anxious about going out and jumping at even familiar everyday noises. With fireworks now easily available all year round, they are also very often let off as part of less predictable festivities such as family birthdays and anniversaries, as well as having become customary in recent years at Christmas and New Year.

We have both owned dogs who were terrified of fireworks, and like you, each year used to dread the approach of the firework season - until we found ways of successfully helping our pets to cope. In this book we aim to share our own personal experiences so that you too can help your cherished companion.

2
WHY IS YOUR DOG SCARED?

While we tend to take loud noises in our stride, the same isn't always true for our dogs. Sudden, unexpected and loud noises will often startle most dogs to some degree, but fireworks can be particularly difficult for many to deal with; don't dismiss it as being wussiness – they really can provoke a genuine fear response. Such fears can occur in any dog, of any breed, and at any age – and sometimes they may develop even though in previous years your pet has appeared unconcerned. Sometimes they are created or reinforced by the behaviour of humans in the household or other pets who may exhibit anxiety; other possible reasons may include:

Physical sensitivity
Even though at the time of writing there are set legal limits in the UK of 120 decibels for shop-bought fireworks, the noise they make is still incredibly loud, as well as occurring at unpredictable intervals and

very often over a prolonged period of time during the evening. As with people, the degree of sensitivity can vary between individuals and will often decline with age, but generally most dogs have far more sensitive hearing than us. They can hear at roughly four times the distance that humans can, and are able to detect much higher frequency noises, such as those produced by 'silent' dog whistles and sonic noise deterrents.

Consequently, in addition to the alarm factor created by unexpected, unfamiliar and very loud noises, the pitch of some fireworks may actually be physically uncomfortable for your dog.

Noise sensitivity

It doesn't take a genius to work out that fireworks are likely to be terrifying for any dog which is noise-sensitive and afraid of everyday sounds such as vacuum cleaners, car alarms and sirens, lawnmowers or even a dropped plate or saucepan lid. It's not always the case, but noise sensitivity can be a consequence of restricted early learning – hence the importance for breeders to try and introduce as many novel experiences as possible early on in a puppy's life, and for the owner of a new puppy to continue that work. Of course, it is also essential that such experiences are introduced in the right way too, or a problem may be created rather than prevented.

There is plenty of scientific evidence to support the fact that the experiences a puppy has in early life really does make a huge difference to his emotional development and that those which lack socialization and habituation to everyday activities, sights and sounds are much more likely to grow into fearful adults. Whilst owners will be responsible for undertaking most of the task of introducing their new pup to as many new things as possible up to the age of 18 months, the period between 4-8 weeks old when the puppy is still with his mother and siblings is particularly critical. During this time he will be especially receptive to new experiences, and any good or bad events which occur will leave an indelible mark on his development, determining the kind of adult he will become. This means that the whole process of socialization and habituation ideally needs to be begun by the breeder if puppies are to get the best start in life. If you are planning on getting a new pup, add asking what work has been done in this respect to your list of questions for the breeder when viewing a litter!

Ensuring plenty of toys and food bowls are available will help to minimise competitiveness over resources between littermates; introducing unfamiliar people (including well-behaved children if available) will also be beneficial. If kennelled outdoors, bringing them into the house will help begin to accustom them to a household environment - even if this can only be managed for short periods, it's better than not at all.

These may seem fairly obvious things to introduce the puppies to, but getting used to a variety of different noises is an equally important, but sometimes overlooked part of the habituation process if future problems are to be prevented. Dogs which do not experience a wide range of different sounds during puppyhood are at risk of developing excessive sensitivity to sound which as well as being a problem in itself, can lead to other issues. A dog which is nervous in traffic for example, will find it harder to feel comfortable when meeting new people or other dogs on the street which can then potentially lead to problems of aggression or unsociability.

The more confident a youngster is with different noises then, the better he will be able to deal with everyday events when the time comes for him to go to his new home, but it is not always easy to expose him to all the noises he may ultimately be likely to encounter. Many puppies are reared in quiet rural locations, and if they end up living in a busy family home in a noisy town it can be tough for them to cope; and on taking the puppy home, new owners may also be limited as to the sights and sounds they can introduce him to until the initial vaccination programme has been completed.

These difficulties can be overcome however by using a good quality sound recording, which enables puppies to be introduced to a wide variety of everyday sounds from very early on in their lives. Ideally it should be played daily from the age of 3 weeks to around 14 weeks old, so it is helpful if new owners continue to use it in the new home. As with a desensitization programme, it is introduced gradually, reaching realistic – not extreme - volumes after a few days. Typical everyday noises which we take for granted but which can be new and scary for a puppy encountering them for the first time might include phones ringing, vacuum cleaners, washing machines and other domestic appliances; as well as these and other household noises a good selection of outdoor ones should be included too such as traffic, aircraft, gardening and DIY noises.

If you have acquired a dog which is noise-sensitive, don't despair: it may be possible to do a lot to reduce his anxiety, and you may find much of the advice given in this book valuable in helping him to cope.

Lack of confidence

A nervous dog is generally an unhappy, apprehensive individual, who lives in a state of constant anxiety, is easily startled and liable to be alarmed by unexpected and/or loud noises.

Although it is most common in dogs which have been poorly socialized and habituated when young, loss of confidence can occur in others for many reasons including insensitive handling and training.

Don't assume that because a dog is large or boisterous he is brimming over with self-assurance or lacks sensitivity – very often the reverse is true. Developing confidence and strengthening bonds of mutual trust between you may therefore be key to helping your dog to cope with fireworks.

Traumatic event

Dogs can become frightened if they have suffered a particularly traumatic experience, which can then cause them to have a sudden onset of fearful behaviour when hearing anything which sounds in any way similar to the original noise.

Life changes

If you have rehomed a dog, you may find that you have also inherited a noise sensitivity problem.

While this may have been an issue which previously existed, it can also start as a result of the upheaval and change of environment and owner.

Because dogs are very sensitive to emotionally charged atmospheres, an owner going through a rough patch can also sometimes be a contributory factor to a dog suddenly developing a fear of fireworks and possibly other phobias, as can any change in your circumstances which leads to you feeling emotional or becoming overprotective of your pet.

Ageing
Unless totally deaf (when the problem often disappears) older dogs - just like people - seem to find it harder to tolerate loud noises, and with some this may develop into fearful behaviours. Some may begin to exhibit these behavioural changes long before they begin to show more obvious physical signs of ageing.

Health issues
There are certain medical conditions which can contribute to, or cause a dog to become noise sensitive – back and hip problems, undiagnosed ear infections and the onset of arthritis for example, are commonly seen in pets with this issue. Sometimes dogs with reduced or loss of vision may become noise sensitive. Noise sensitivity and fearfulness can also be linked to hypothyroidism: complete thyroid profiling can help determine whether this is the case. Before you try doing anything else to address the fear of fireworks, you should therefore *always* first get your pet checked out by a vet.

Early neutering
With the growing trend for early neutering of our pets, behaviourists and vets are seeing an increase in anxiety problems in dogs. These have been linked in studies to the adrenal gland over-producing the 'flight or fight' stress hormone cortisol. This can lead to dogs exhibiting fear aggression and separation anxiety as well as noise phobia.

No known causes
Fears are often irrational, and although sometimes a

dog's fear of fireworks can be traced to a particular experience, sometimes there is no obvious trigger – or nothing which is obvious to you at any rate, and since your dog can't talk, he can't tell you. Sometimes signs of distress will develop in an otherwise placid and confident pet, and this can be particularly baffling for owners if the dog has appeared calm and unworried on previous occasions.

What *is* certain is that whether your pet has been fearful of fireworks in previous years, or if he has only just started to exhibit signs of anxiety, he will continue to be fearful again in the future unless you take steps to resolve the problem. And even if you aren't expecting fireworks for many months yet, it's never too soon to start working on the problem.

3
CAN ANYTHING BE DONE?

Fearfulness of fireworks appears to be a growing problem: according to a recent Dogs Trust survey, around 72% of dogs are affected, with 1 in 10 being so severely traumatized that veterinary attention has been required. Another study in the US estimates that around 23 million dogs there are adversely affected. Such figures indicate that it is a large and widespread problem, and until the rather unlikely event of firework sales to the general public becoming banned comes about, it is one which is not going to go away in the immediately foreseeable future. This makes it all the more important that you can take positive steps to reduce the amount of stress caused to your pet.

Spotting the signs
If your dog is scared, you may notice various signs of distress which may range from mild to severe, including:

- Trembling and shaking
- Being very clingy, sticking closely to you
- Cowering
- Tail tucking
- Pacing
- Running around
- Trying to escape through doors, windows (and even cat flaps)
- Hiding behind or under furniture
- Crying, whining, barking, howling
- Rapid lip licking, panting, drooling

Some dogs can also become destructive, or even aggressive, and may urinate, defecate or be afflicted with diarrhoea. These are all more obvious indicators, but in milder cases there may be more subtle and less apparent signs which are overlooked or perhaps dismissed as just a bit of naughtiness.

Spending time observing your dog both at home and out and about will help you to become familiar with his body language so that you know what is 'normal', confident behaviour for him and when he is acting out of character. Being able to pick up those more subtle indications that he is not entirely comfortable with something will stand you in good stead in a wide variety of other situations too – and of course, the earlier that you can spot that something is wrong, the more successful you are likely to be in resolving it.

Learning to 'read' your dog can be tremendously rewarding and is a skill well worth developing, as it will help you to develop a more intuitive, richer and more fulfilling relationship with him.

It will also help you to determine the safest, most appropriate way of interacting with him at all times, as well as in deciding on the most suitable course of action to take in helping him to overcome his fears. Body language is a fascinating but complex topic which is too large to cover in sufficient detail here, but you will find some suggestions for further reading on this subject in the Resources section at the end of this book.

Taking action

If your dog is one of the millions who are fearful of fireworks there are many ways in which you can actively help him to cope with, and sometimes even to successfully overcome his fears completely. If you know that he has a problem, don't wait for the firework season to begin to start addressing it. Even if your dog currently shows only a very mild level of concern, you still need to start taking action straightaway as fear tends to escalate, becoming worse on each successive occasion and making it much harder to resolve.

As you will discover in the following pages, there are plenty of things you can do. You may find that you need to adopt several of the suggestions here rather than relying on just a single one. Some may require more time and effort on your part than others, but if you care about your pet, you won't begrudge it. Over time you may find that from simply helping him to cope on the night initially, his anxiety begins to diminish and may even vanish altogether, but don't expect to cure your dog overnight. It can be a long term process, and where fears are very deeply entrenched or other factors apply, you may not be able to eliminate them completely: but even so, you can do a lot to make the situation one which he is better able to tolerate.

As with any behavioural issue, no matter how trying it may be for you, remember that it is much, much worse for your pet. Never attempt to force him to face up to things that frighten him, as you'll lose his trust in you and he'll just become more frightened. Any loss of temper on your part is also likely to set him back.

As we mentioned earlier, before doing anything else, do take your dog to the vet to be thoroughly checked over for any health issues. If he is severely phobic, we would also recommend that after a vet check, you seek help from an experienced animal behaviour counsellor or Tellington TTouch practitioner on referral from your vet.

Be aware that the breadth, level and depth of knowledge and practical experience of those who advertise their services as 'counsellors' or 'trainers' can be variable; anyone can give themselves these titles and even if someone has good credentials on paper, may lack hands-on skills. Check them out thoroughly before enlisting their services and satisfy yourself that anyone you consult works in a humane and compassionate manner, using only positive training methods. You will find some helpful information on what to look for and how to find someone in your area who may be able to help on the Association of Pet Dog Trainers (APDT) website. Contact details for the APDT, Association of Pet Behaviour Counsellors (APBC) and Tellington TTouch Practitioners can be found at the end of this book.

4
YOUR 10 POINT PLAN
FOR THE NIGHT

Check if, where, and when public displays are being held in your neighbourhood, so that you have a rough idea of when the noises are likely to be at their peak. Don't forget to ask your neighbours to let you know if they are planning any home firework displays. In addition to adopting one or more of the suggestions on the following pages, you can then set up a 10 point plan to help reduce stress and minimise the risk of accident or injury on nights when fireworks are expected. Make sure that all the members of your household are familiar with it.

1.

Every year many dogs are injured, go missing or are killed as a result of fireworks being set off while they are out walking with their owners. In some countries there may be a curfew on fireworks: in the UK, current legislation sets this between the hours of

11pm and 7am, with a much later one on certain specific days: midnight on Bonfire Night, and 1am on Diwali, New Year and Chinese New Year. Unfortunately these curfews are not always observed, and sometimes fireworks are also illegally set off in public areas or during daylight, so whatever the time, it is a sensible precaution to keep your dog on a leash when walking him during the firework season.

Take your dog for his main walk while it is still light, and out again to toilet before dusk falls and fireworks can be expected to start, as it may be some time before it is safe to venture outside for him to relieve himself again. Wait until well after the suggested finish time before taking your dog for his final toileting break before bed. If he refuses to go out or you can still hear bangs going on, get up a couple of hours earlier than usual the next morning to let him out.

Do not be tempted to go out for a last late night walk when you think all the fireworks have stopped. Very often another one – or more - goes off when you are least expecting it, and a change in routine for a few days is far preferable to increasing your dog's anxieties. If you aren't fortunate enough to have a garden, do not go any further from your front door, or stay out any longer than is necessary for your pet to relieve himself; this can be one of those occasions when it is handy to have taught your dog a toilet cue so you can encourage him to get on with things promptly. We have included a step by step guide below in case you are unsure of how to go about it.

How to teach a pee cue:

Teaching your dog a 'pee command' is simple to train and can be really useful. It can help him to know what you expect of him, when and where. Once learned, it will mean you will no longer have to stand in the rain or cold for ages waiting for him to empty his bladder last thing at night, or if you take him away on holiday and he is not sure if or where he is allowed to go. It also enables you to ensure he has relieved himself before setting out on car journeys, or visiting other people's gardens.

- Think of a word that you want to use as your pee cue. The most common words or phrases used are 'busy, busy' or 'hurry up', but you can choose whatever you like, as long as it is something you don't use often during everyday life, and which won't be embarrassing for you, or offensive to others, to use in public.

- Whenever you take your dog out on a walk, or into the garden to toilet, wait until you see him actually peeing; only once he is in full flow say your chosen pee cue eg 'Busy, busy' or 'hurry up' and keep repeating it until he is done.

- Once he has finished give him a huge amount of praise and a yummy treat (make sure you have remembered to take the treat out with you!) It is important that you give him the treat there and then so he makes the connection between the action and reward.

- Repeat this stage for a few days; you will find that you soon learn to recognise the visual cues he gives, just before he starts to toilet. Now is the time to introduce your pee cue, just before, or right as, he starts to go. Be sure that he is definitely about to start before you use the verbal cue though, or he won't make the connection between the word and the action. Do keep rewarding and heaping on the praise as he finishes.

- After a few more days, try giving the command when he looks as though he might be interested in going; give the pee cue and repeat it as he goes, praising lavishly and rewarding with a treat as he finishes, just as you have done previously. If you have misjudged matters, don't worry; simply repeat the earlier steps to establish more firmly the association between the pee cue and action and to give you more time to learn the little giveaway signs that he wants, or is about, to spend a penny.
- Eventually, you will be able to say the word and it will encourage him to toilet; do continue to reward, with praise and/or a treat, even after he knows the command, to reinforce the behaviour. Some dogs are very quick to pick this cue up, while others can take a little longer to catch on; but all dogs can be taught it, regardless of age.

If you do have a garden, don't assume that it is escape proof. If your dog needs to go outside do not send him out there alone – go with him, and no matter how good your fences are, keep him on a lead, even if things seem to have gone quiet. A dog which is crazed with fear can succeed in breaking out from the most secure of areas, and may possibly injure himself badly in the process.

If you have an interconnecting door to your garage you may be able to set up an alternative toileting area for your dog over the firework period. You can use a child's paddling pool or something waterproof on the ground and place turf, artificial grass or puppy training pads over the top. If your dog is initially reluctant to use the area, use your cue word for toileting if you have taught one, or even collect some of his urine to sprinkle on the area to encourage use. Start to train him to use the area a few weeks in advance so he is familiar with it. You could first place it outside and reward him for peeing in the right place and then start to move it inside the garage. It will cut down his anxiety of running the gauntlet in the garden for his last late-night pee.

If you think this all sounds excessively cautious, think again: more dogs get lost on 5th November in the UK and 4th July in the US – both big firework occasions – than on any other date in the year. And even if your dog has never demonstrated any fear of fireworks in the past, it doesn't mean that the same will hold true this year, so you should make every effort to keep him safe.

2.

Don't leave your dog at home alone - or shut away in a separate room from you either, except very briefly if you need to answer the front door to a caller, in order to prevent him from being able to escape outside past you. If he can be in the same room as you, he will feel safer. Ensure that you have done all the necessary jobs for yourself so that you don't have to leave him in order to carry out activities such as cooking and showering. You will then be able to monitor him closely and provide reassurance and support if it is needed.

3.

Make sure your dog wears a collar with an ID tag and is microchipped with all the contact details up to date, just in case the worst happens and he escapes and runs off in fright when the loud noises start.

4.

Stick to normal routines as much as possible. Where you need to change them slightly – for example to fit in exercise and meals at times when it will be quiet – start to adjust them gradually and well in advance, as abrupt changes to routine can in itself be stressful for some dogs. Make sure that you feed your dog well before any bangs are due to start.

5.

As soon as it begins to get dark outside, shut all windows and draw all curtains to block out any scary flashes of light and muffle the sounds of fireworks. If you don't have curtains or if you have blinds, hanging blankets over the windows will increase the sound-dampening effect. If you don't have curtain rails, you can drape them over spring-loaded tension rods which are non-permanent, easy to set up and require no DIY skills to fit.

6.

Double check that all windows and external doors are shut. If you have a cat or dog flap, make sure it is securely blocked up to prevent escape attempts. Fear doesn't encourage rational thinking, so even though the fireworks are outside, a terrified dog may still attempt to run out there, and once in the middle of it all will then panic even further. Leave internal house doors open however, so your dog doesn't feel trapped, and has access to his favourite denning area if he has one. If he does want to den up, allow him to retreat but check on him occasionally. You will find more information on setting up a den for your dog to use in the following pages.

7.

If your dog is settled and calm when the bangs start, leave him to his own devices.

Do not draw his attention to what is going on outside by looking in the direction of the noise, holding your breath or reacting in any other way than you would during a normal evening.

8.

Keep an eye on the level of the drinking bowl, as anxious dogs tend to pant more and so will get thirsty and drink more than usual.

9.

It is okay to be proactive and get hands-on with your dog: it is not necessary to ignore fearful behaviour, as is sometimes advised. Spend ten to twenty minutes doing some Tellington TTouch body work on your dog before all the bangs begin and slip a body wrap or Thundershirt on him for the duration of the evening. Once the noise starts, if he becomes upset but is staying near you, offer some more TTouches, ensuring that you are matter-of-fact about it. You will not make his reaction worse by doing body work at this time. You will find more detailed information about Tellington TTouch, body wraps, Thundershirts and how to use them in the following pages.

10.

Do be aware of your own personal safety, that of others and of your dog at all times. Always bear in mind that a frightened dog may behave out of character.

5
WHAT TO DO
IF YOU GET GAUGHT OUTSIDE
WHEN ALL THE BANGS START

It can be one of the most heart-stopping moments for an owner if you get caught outside with your dog when a firework goes off. Some dogs may bolt in blind terror, while others may lie down and refuse to move – but even if you think your dog is fine with fireworks, it is important for his own safety as well as that of others, that you walk him on a leash and do not allow him to run loose while there is any likelihood of fireworks going off. Bear in mind that sometimes mischief makers will let off a firework or two during daylight hours, so do not assume that this is a safe time to exercise your pet.

Make sure that whatever the leash is attached to is escape-proof; using both a collar and a harness with a connecting link between them, and a double-ended leash which can be attached to both will give you a little extra security. However, a frightened dog can back out of a collar, even if it is tightly adjusted, and many 'bikini-top' style harnesses aren't foolproof either. The best and most effective solution is to fit a 'belt and braces' type of harness – basically this involves an extra strap which fits around the narrowest part of your dog's tuck-up. You can either buy one or adapt an existing harness as shown in Pic 1 below.

Pic 1: An existing harness can easily be adapted to make it escape proof *(image courtesy of Toni Shelbourne)*

This will be impossible for your dog to wiggle out of and has the additional benefit that no damage will be caused to the neck should your dog get into a panic and throw himself around. Contrary to certain popular opinions, if your dog is taught to walk properly when on a leash, a harness will not encourage him to pull! You may find various harnesses of the self-tightening variety advertised as being escape proof as well as discouraging pulling: in our opinion these are best avoided. It is not necessary to inflict discomfort to keep your dog safely contained or to teach him to walk nicely on the leash.

Even if you rely solely on a harness to walk your dog in, he should still wear a correctly fitted collar carrying an ID tag – if he gets lost, this is usually the first place that whoever finds him will look. In addition to helping you to be quickly reunited should the unthinkable happen and he gets loose, it is compulsory under UK law when in any public place. As well as wearing an ID tag on his collar, make sure your dog is microchipped, and that the details on both forms of identification are correct and up to date.

If you would like to give your dog a little more freedom you can use a long line. Using one is a skill in itself, and both you and your dog should be familiar with it; don't try it out for the first time during the firework season! You should only ever use it attached to a harness, never directly to the collar, again to avoid the risk of damage to the neck should he suddenly take off.

Do **not** use an extending lead as these give you very little control over your dog, can cause serious injuries to dog and handler, and can be difficult to keep hold of in emergency situations when an abrupt tug from your dog can yank the handle right out of your hand. The sight and sound of it bouncing along behind your dog may scare him even more, and make it even more difficult to catch him.

While out on leash walks, putting a Thundershirt or body wrap on your dog may give him added confidence and reassurance. You'll find more information about these two pieces of equipment and how to use them later on in the book.

Before venturing out it is also a good idea to dress your dog in a hi-vis jacket of some kind as this will make it easier for you to spot him and motorists to avoid him should you accidentally become separated from each other. These and other visibility aids such as blinking lights that can be attached to his collar and harness can be bought from online and high street pet shop retailers.

If fireworks do unexpectedly go off while you are out, wait until they have stopped and if you have introduced some of the Tellington TTouches at home, you can then do some, choosing ones such as the Zebra, Springbok and Ear work to start with. After a few minutes, even if your dog still seems agitated move on again and continue your walk, although it may be wise to cut it shorter than usual in case other fireworks are let off. You don't have to wait until a scary noise upsets your sensitive dog though: stopping in a quiet area for a few minutes during your walk and doing some TTouches may make it easier for him to cope in the event of an unanticipated bang.

Should the worst happen and despite all your precautions your dog does get loose either while you are walking him, or by escaping from your garden or house, make sure you know the correct procedure to follow.

Do not waste time wondering if he will eventually wander back of his own accord. Contact local veterinary practices, kennels, animal rescue shelters, dog wardens and the police, in case your dog is found and handed over to them by a member of the public. You might also like to go online and contact **www.doglost.co.uk** which will be able to offer advice and help you to organise a search.

Organise friends and relatives to help you search, allocating everyone an area so that time isn't wasted looking in the same place twice. Make sure someone stays at home just in case your dog does return there, and so they can answer the phone and co-ordinate all the searchers.

Use social media too, posting details and asking for assistance in case there are any sightings. It is worth covering a wide area, as a dog which is in a blind panic will often travel far and fast.

It is likely that when he does finally slow down, he may hide somewhere so he may be difficult to find. Even if he hears the voice of someone he knows he may be reluctant to leave any place of safety he has found. If one of the search party does discover him however, unless it is a person he knows very well and trusts completely, they should simply keep an eye on him, making no move to alarm him, and call for you to come and catch him.

If you still have not found him by the next day, continue to contact vets, kennels, rescue organisations, dog wardens and the police on a daily basis as they may not immediately make the connection with you, especially if he has lost his collar ID. Make sure you give them a very good description and if possible supply them with a clear recent photo as they may not always be familiar with breeds, and if he is a cross breed may have even more trouble identifying him.

A good description is essential since although microchipping is a good way of proving ownership and of effecting a speedy return of your pet if he is found, you should be aware that very occasionally the chips do fail, and that stray dogs are not always routinely scanned when they are handed in. Do support the

Vets Get Scanning campaign in the UK to try and help change this situation! Details can be found at the end of this book.

6
HELPING YOUR DOG

Lifestyle changes – Setting an example – Diversion – Creating a den – Soundproofing – Comfort food – Lighting – Company – Background noise – Exercise – Medication – Holistic options – Desensitization – Adaptil – Tellington TTouch

Even though all your special preparations for the night (or nights) are in place, perhaps your dog is still hiding in the downstairs cloakroom, or trying to squeeze behind the settee or beneath the bed. Or maybe he is barking frantically, or trying to dig up the carpet, or losing control of his bladder or bowels … in extreme cases some dogs may even become aggressive as their owners try to restrain them. Many lose out on their evening walks, too scared to leave the house until morning and even then are jumpy and difficult to walk.

But don't despair as there are many ways in which you can help your dog. Some may work better with one individual than with another, so be prepared to be adaptable in your approach; there is no such thing

27

as a 'one size fits all' solution when it comes to addressing any problem whether emotional, psychological or physical. You may also find that for maximum success you will need to combine several of the suggestions offered here.

Try to take a long-term view: although management and short-term coping strategies can be both valuable and necessary, if you are prepared to do a little work on a regular basis it is possible to make more profound and lasting changes which will benefit your dog in all areas of his life, as well as in this more specific one. It is important to be realistic in your expectations though: sometimes you will see an enormous improvement, but with some dogs it may not be possible to completely 'cure' them of their fear of fireworks.

But being able to do something which can make the situation more tolerable for both of you is certainly better than doing nothing, and even when any initial improvement is only small, it is at least a step in the right direction and if you persevere you will very often find that your dog's ability to deal with the issue grows with each successive year.

LIFESTYLE CHANGES

Many noise-sensitive dogs tend to be stressed dogs in general, so an important part of remedying the problem may require you to look in detail at, and be prepared to change, various aspects of his lifestyle, such as his food; changing to a very natural, additive-free diet for example, can often improve matters with anxious dogs. As well as food, you may need to explore a whole range of other things, including exercise, how you and other members of the family interact with your dog, training, grooming and other areas of daily care.

It can be useful to enlist the help of an animal counsellor or Tellington TTouch practitioner to aid you in pinpointing possible areas where making changes might be of benefit to your dog. Doing so is not a reflection on your experience or ability to look after your dog well – it is simply that it can be difficult for an owner to take an objective view of their own pet, and thus very easy to overlook potential stressors.

Building confidence levels generally, and helping your dog to feel more self-assured in everyday life will be beneficial, and should be an ongoing process. Many noise-sensitive dogs have other underlying fears and anxieties and may be so stressed that when really scary events happen they then find it impossible to cope.

Tellington TTouch Training is brilliant for developing confidence; it is also invaluable in cultivating and strengthening trust and the bond between you and your pet, so that he is more likely to respond to your calm example. Tellington TTouch is explained in more detail later in this book: you can also discover more about it by visiting the websites listed at the end of this book.

SETTING AN EXAMPLE

Try to act normally and not to react to your dog's distress, as any concern you show will tend to reinforce his fears rather than reassure him. Not reacting to his anxieties doesn't mean that you need to go to the opposite extreme and ignore him completely however, and speaking reassuringly and soothingly to him, and providing distractions (see page 31) may help in mild cases. Much as you might want to, avoid actually cuddling him however, as some dogs may find being restricted in such a way hard to cope with when they are feeling panicky and may snap at you. A more helpful and safer way of interacting with him, is by using the special Tellington TTouch body work called 'TTouches' to help calm and reassure him; more about these later.

Dogs are very much aware of, and tuned into, body language so try to avoid holding your breath, staring at your dog or generally being anxious yourself when you hear a noise. Shouting and becoming upset, frustrated or angry will also be counterproductive; even though it may be directed against those letting off the fireworks rather than directly at your dog, he won't understand this.

Because your dog will watch and mirror your attitude, giving 'calming signals' can help to influence his behaviour in frightening situations. Yawning and lip licking *can* be signs of stress; but done the right way they can also let your dog know that there's nothing to worry about. The key lies in the speed, or rather in the lack of it, during these actions: lick your lips *slowly*, and yawn in a very *slow*, sleepy way: also try some *slow* blinking, and generally try to keep all your movements *slow* and relaxed.

If you notice your dog staring at you, drop your chin and look slowly away, maybe giving a small, relaxed yawn as you do so or take a deep breath and exhale slowly.

For new puppies or first-time firework season dogs, an owner being really excited and asking in an excited voice, "What's that" and linking the bangs with a positive association like food, can really help. Toni knows dogs who have had this method used with them who will even go in the garden to watch the pretty lights!

DIVERSION

It may be possible to divert your pet's attention from what is going on outdoors by offering some kind of edible treat; this may need to be especially tasty, depending on the level of noise happening outside. Treats which are long lasting and involve chewing are best for providing an outlet for anxiety, as the action of chewing releases endorphins – these are chemicals produced by the brain, which can help him to cope with stress.

Depending on your dog's preferences and what he is used to, this could be either a raw meaty bone or a Kong tightly stuffed with goodies for him to tease out. Kongs are pyramidal cylinders made of flexible but tough rubber: make sure you buy one which is of the right size and robustness for your pet. Introduce it to him on a number of occasions during the weeks leading up to firework nights: pack the contents loosely to start with and as he becomes more expert at extracting them, begin to stuff the contents more tightly so that it becomes more challenging and requires more nibbling, chewing and licking. Freezing wet food or a meaty broth inside it can also make it last a satisfyingly long time. Give it to him *before* you expect to hear any noise outside, so that he is already busily occupied. More information about choosing the right Kong and ideas for filling them can be found in the Contacts and Resources section.

Other good diversions include the various hollow toys with small openings which treats can be inserted into and which need to be teased out, Snuffelmats, or the 'puzzle solving' games such as those marketed by Nina Ottosson. Depending on your pet, it may be best however, to avoid the type of toy which involves vigorous rolling or batting around to release the treats (such as pyramids and activity cubes and balls), as these may increase excitement levels.

Be careful in your choice of treats as some commercial products may contain ingredients which create undesirable levels of excitability. There are plenty which are additive-free, and some which also contain ingredients, such as oats, chamomile and passion-flower, that are said to help relax your pet. You could of course, always bake your own: refer to the Further Reading section for canine recipe books.

You could also try having a game with your dog, although avoid chasing/rough and tumble/tuggy type games which can be very exciting and may raise levels of adrenalin still higher. Try involving him instead in hide and seek or nosework games which require intense mental concentration and are absorbing, but not excessively physically stimulating.

If you work at developing your dog's interest in food and toys on an everyday basis, you will be able to use them more successfully on such occasions. Having said that, these options are only likely to work if the level of anxiety present is very mild, and may be less useful with highly stressed dogs.

Brief training sessions may be another way of creating a diversion. Stick to things your dog already knows how to do and use high motivation treats as rewards in the same way as you would when training in a new place or where there are lots of distractions. As well as giving him something to do, this sort of activity will also help to keep your dog focussed on you being calm. The more tricks your dog knows, the more you can do with him, so try to add to your dog's repertoire throughout the year: check the Further Reading section for books which will give you a few new ideas. In addition to training exercises and games, you could also try setting up an indoor 'Confidence Course' – you'll find more details about this later on in the book.

Bear in mind that your dog may not be able to perform at as high a standard as usual so do not be too demanding: be prepared to be easily satisfied and quick to reward. Remember that the object is to distract him rather than to perfect exercises. Don't persist if your dog's stress levels are so high that he cannot concentrate on what you are asking – it may in fact increase them if he feels that he is failing.

CREATING A DEN

Many dogs like to hide in a den when they are scared, which is why they will often try to climb into cupboards, squeeze into tight spots under furniture, or even pull up carpets to try and squirm beneath.

If your dog has a favoured denning place which he already uses such as under a bed or in the cupboard under the stairs, let him carry on using it provided that it's safe for him to do so. If you need to encourage him to relocate elsewhere, it's usually easiest to provide a crate, although you can improvise at a pinch with a pop-up tent, a table or even a couple of chairs pushed together with a blanket thrown over the top. Available from pet shops or online, crates may be made of steel mesh or soft fabric, and will fold up flat when not in use so they are easy to store. Alternatively, a rigid plastic pet carrier is just as good, if more awkward to store when not in use. Whatever sort you choose, it should however, be big enough for him to stand up, lie down and turn round in comfortably.

Set up and introduce the crate at least a month before the first fireworks are expected so that your dog is familiar with it and likes being in it. If he has a preferred room which he generally goes to at times of stress, set it up in there. Otherwise, choose the quietest room which has the fewest windows facing towards where the fireworks are likely to be going off.

Put some comfy bedding inside, feed him in it, and pop treats and toys in there to make it a cosy and inviting place which has pleasant associations and where he will voluntarily choose to spend time relaxing. Always leave the door open so that he can come and go as he wishes; don't shut him in, as the object is to provide him with a place where he feels safe, not trapped. Covering the crate with a blanket will help to increase the feeling of security; it will also make it dimmer inside and help to muffle external noises.

On the night itself, leave the choice of using the den to your dog: never try and force him into it or lock him in, as he might injure himself or destroy the crate in his frantic attempts to escape if he panics.

Sometimes your dog may decide to use a completely different denning area rather than the one that you have carefully set up and encouraged him to use during the preceding months and weeks. Go with the flow if that's where your dog feels safest. Never pull him out of safe areas, as this may prove physically dangerous for you as well as being distressing for your dog.

If you have a dog that likes to dig, then as an alternative to a den, you could try setting up a big pile of blankets and duvets in the room that he can burrow into and under. Some dogs, as well as owners, seem to find weighted therapy blankets comforting to snuggle beneath: these can be bought in various weights, so if giving one a try, choose something appropriate to his size and build. Different materials are used by manufacturers to provide the 'weight', ranging from ceramic coated metal discs to polypropylene pellets and glass micro beads. It goes without saying that these could be harmful should your dog become destructive and start to tear at or chew on the blanket, so he should not be left unsupervised with it.

SOUNDPROOFING

Two sound proof crates are currently on the market which aim to provide a quiet refuge. The ZenCrate in the US and The Quiet Kennel in the UK both claim to help reduce anxiety linked to noise phobia; both are also somewhat expensive so it might be worth keeping an eye on reviews and waiting for the prices to come down before thinking of purchasing.

It is also possible to buy 'Mutt Muffs' - ear muffs designed for dogs, but feedback about them is mixed. The main problem seems to be that they can be shaken off easily, and you would need a pretty tolerant dog to accept them. We do know of several people who have had some success with the rather cheaper option of dog snoods, which help both to dampen down the noise and aid in calming the response to fireworks. They should be made of a stretchy fabric so they follow the contours of your dog's head and neck, and although a close fit, should be a comfortable one and not tight. Knitted or fleece doggy snoods are often a popular item on sighthound websites and charity auctions (although sold for warmth rather than as ear defenders) or you can easily improvise your own from a legwarmer or woolly sock with the toe cut off, depending on the size of your dog.

If you try either of these options, take time to accustom your dog well in advance, taking things slowly, noting his response and following the same general guidelines as when introducing a Body wrap or Thundershirt. Do not leave your dog in them while unsupervised.

COMFORT FOOD

It is fairly well documented that diet, in both humans and dogs can have a dramatic influence on behaviour as well as health. Precisely what constitutes a healthy and appropriate diet is a matter of much controversy, frequently provoking passionate and often heated debate: what all opinions do agree on however, is that products containing artificial preservatives, antioxidants and food colourings are generally best avoided. Artificial colourings in particular have been linked to hyperactivity.

Depending on what you feed your dog then, his diet has the potential to enhance calmness or aggravate behavioural issues. If you feed a commercially prepared diet, choose one which is of good quality, but even so, read the labelling carefully. It can sometimes be confusing and ambiguous, so you may need to do a little extra research to find out more about the ingredients listed, or to help you understand what the information on those labels really means – and equally importantly, what has been left out.

Feed your dog at least one hour before you expect to hear any fireworks, because once they start he may become too anxious to eat. For most dogs, missing an occasional meal may not be too much of a big deal; but if, for example, he needs to take medication with food, it can be more of an issue and it may be wise to start changing evening meal and medication times in advance of the start of the firework season.

Giving a meal which contains plenty of carbohydrate, such as pasta or rice, may encourage him to sleep, but again add this to the diet slowly over a week or so and take care if your dog has food intolerances.

Keep an eye on his figure during this time of year as some dogs may lose weight due to stress while others may pile on a few unwanted pounds if you are adding pasta or giving extra treats as a diversion.

Calming supplements

Tryptophan is an essential amino acid found in foods such as red meat, eggs, fish and poultry. It is converted in the brain into serotonin, a neurotransmitter involved in sleep, mood and sensitivity, producing feelings of contentment, relaxation and pleasure, so has gained a reputation as being beneficial in promoting calmness. You may like to try either a commercial diet which has increased levels of tryptophan added to it, or to augment your current good quality food with a tryptophan supplement.

Oatmeal is another foodstuff which is claimed to have a calming effect on the nervous system as it is high in B vitamins, which can play an important part in emotional wellbeing and combatting the effects of stress. Incidentally, vitamin B6 also plays an important role in the synthesis of serotonin and the metabolism of tryptophan to serotonin.

You can add cooked oatmeal (don't use the instant sort) to meals - just cook a little extra in the mornings when making porridge for yourself, making it with water rather than milk as some dogs are lactose intolerant, and leaving out the salt and any flavourings. It may seem on the bland side to you, but most dogs love it. Alternatively you can make oat tea by steeping a tablespoonful of oatmeal in a cup of hot water for twenty minutes and once it has cooled, adding it to kibble or biscuit meal several times a week. You might also like to grow a pot of oat grass - *Avena sativa*, often labelled on seed packets as 'cat grass' - which your dog can help himself to, grazing on it as and when he wishes.

There are many commercial dietary supplements available which also claim to have a calming effect, containing ingredients ranging from a protein found in cow's milk to B vitamins, tryptophan, and various herbs such as chamomile. Some owners have found them to be helpful, but as always the advice is to always consult your vet first to ensure that the product is suitable for your pet and will not interact adversely with any medication he is taking. Note also that several of these 'calming' supplements state that they should not be given to pregnant or lactating bitches, so read all accompanying information carefully.

With most of these products, the manufacturers suggest that for the best results you should start giving them several days beforehand as well as on the day itself. They are not generally intended for long term use however, and while some owners have reported good results in reducing signs of stress, others have noted little difference. They may be useful to try as a way of helping to support your dog while working through reducing his anxieties about fireworks, but remember that they will not directly address the problem on their own - your dog will continue to be frightened of fireworks.

LIGHTING

Encourage your dog to relax and doze by turning the lights down. The pineal gland in the brain synthesizes and secretes melatonin, which helps induce restfulness and sleep, but this process only takes place at night as the enzymes responsible for producing it are inactivated by light. You don't actually need to sit in pitch darkness (if there are any flashes of light outside which sneak round the edges of your curtains, it will also make them more obvious) but do either dim the lights, or use low-lighting side lights rather than bright overhead ones.

COMPANY

Sometimes dogs are more prepared to follow the lead of another canine, so if you have a friend with a dog which gets on well with yours and isn't bothered by fireworks, you could invite them both round to help set the right example to your pet. However this can work both ways, and if your dog's anxiety begins to make the other one agitated, send him home early. For this reason, you should not consider getting a second dog in the hope that he will help the first one to settle, as very often he will simply pick up on his fears and then you will have double the trouble, with two scared dogs to deal with instead of one.

Ultimately, it is you or other trusted members of the family who are the most important company for your dog. You may have to create a rota so that there is always at least one person home with him. If you work late and get home after dark you may have to ask a friend or family member to come round to sit with your dog until you return.

BACKGROUND NOISE

Music can have a beneficial calming effect on both you and your dog. For preference use recordings rather than the TV or radio, as it will give you more choice and greater control over what you listen to.

Classical music has been shown in studies to have a soothing and relaxing influence – appropriately enough, Bach has proved to be a favourite – but avoid anything which is too rousing, or has lots of drum rolls or clashing of cymbals. Some people claim that rhythmical music with a strong beat will help to mask any noises outside better, while others swear by jazz. Generally though, instrumental pieces are best, and heavy metal music should be avoided altogether as it tends to have an agitating effect. Pop music on the other hand, seems to have little effect either way. You can also buy 'psychoacoustically designed' music specifically arranged for dogs, and which is alleged to be even more successful in creating a calming atmosphere than conventional classical recordings.

Experiment with different types of music ahead of time in order to discover which your dog prefers and has the most profound effect on him. Once you have made your choice, play it half a dozen times or so when he isn't showing any signs of anxiety. On the day (or days) when fireworks are expected, put it on at least half an hour before you anticipate them starting, and continue to play it throughout the evening.

The volume should be loud enough to help disguise some of the external noise, but not uncomfortable. Another area you might like to try is a white noise machine which can help mask outside noises and

which some owners find very successful; put it on
before you expect any noises to start.

EXERCISE

You may have to change your usual exercise routine
during the firework season. You cannot predict when
or where fireworks will go off, human behaviour or
lack of understanding by inconsiderate people, and
many problems have been created by owners insisting
on taking their dog out for a walk after getting home
from work when it is dark. Instead, it is better to get
up a little earlier in the mornings at this time of year
to give your dog a longer walk when he will have the
chance to run around in safety and work off excess
energy. Avoid elevating epinephrine levels (the neuro-
chemical responsible for the 'flight or fight' response
which occurs when stressed or scared) with wildly
exciting games though. Instead, incorporate lots of
brief training sessions so he is mentally as well as
physically a little tired and likely to be less reactive to
loud noises. Low intensity exercise will actually result
in the lowering of epinephrine levels, while low to
moderate intensity exercise also helps to increase natural levels of serotonin (the brain's 'feelgood' chemical) which produces feelings of calmness and contentment. Furthermore, it beneficially elevates dopa-
mine levels: this is a neurotransmitter which is involved with the wake/sleep cycle, affects emotional
responses and is associated with bonding, attachment
and focussed thinking.

If you live in an area where fireworks are sometimes
let off during the day, play safe and keep your dog on
the leash as discussed earlier in this book.

If there is no alternative, it will not harm your dog if

he misses a few walks at the height of the firework period; better to be safe than sorry. Many dogs may not want to set paw outside in the dark anyway, and if your dog is one of these, please don't force him to go out. You can always play with him indoors if he needs some exercise and you have a safe and big enough area: although do avoid ball games on slippery floors which could lead to injury.

Remember to take him out to toilet before any bangs are likely to start. Late at night, after the fireworks have died down, even if you have a secure garden, accompany your dog outside with a leash on so he can relieve himself. Remember, do not force him to venture outside or get annoyed with him if he is too anxious to do anything while he is out there. Either try again later on, or get up a little earlier the next morning to let him out.

MEDICATION

The field of behavioural medications for dogs has advanced in the last few years and there are various drugs available from your vet which may be helpful in severe cases of noise sensitivity. Sedatives and tranquilisers are not often a useful long-term solution since they do not treat the underlying problem, only mask it, and the pet cannot learn to adapt. Anti-anxiety medication may be more appropriate - integrated into a behaviour programme, it may be the only way to successfully facilitate long-lasting change for severely affected dogs.

It is not a course of action to embark on lightly though: some drugs can have as many disadvantages as benefits. Some are unsuitable for long term use, many have a long list of side effects or simply may not be an option if your dog has certain health issues or is taking other medications.

Discuss the matter at length with your vet: we would suggest asking for a referral to a veterinary behaviourist who will be familiar with the different drugs available to use for noise phobia if your usual vet has limited experience with them. Be prepared to do a little research online of your own, too. The NOAH Compendium of Animal Medicines is a useful online resource for finding out more about known contra-indications and side effects of the various products available. You can search by either product name or active ingredient at: **www.noahcompendium.co.uk**. Look also for reviews and comments from other owners who have used the products you are interested in. As well as highlighting any potential issues for your dog, it can be helpful in preparing a list of questions to ask your vet, and in reassuring yourself that you are making the right decision and choice of medication for your pet.

We would suggest that you do explore all other alternatives first, and consider medication as a last resort rather than a first choice. However, never say never! Drugs alone will rarely solve a severe anxiety problem - but behaviour modification alone may not work either, without the support of medication. With highly phobic dogs it may be necessary to take the pharmaceutical route in order to prevent excessive distress and to make it possible to teach new skills and behaviours. These drugs should be used with the advice and backup of a vet and animal behaviourist working in consultation with each other as a way of helping your dog to cope while working to overcome its fears and make long-lasting change. Paradoxically, there can be unanticipated consequences: a study conducted in the UK indicated that those owners using drugs during desensitization treatment were less inclined to follow the training plan they were given by the behaviourist or to stick to it, resulting in a lower success rate. Be warned, and do not become lazy about following the training!

HOLISTIC OPTIONS

Holistic therapies are becoming increasingly popular for both humans and animals, and in many instances can be very successful. However, you should always remember that just because a product is labelled as being 'natural' or 'holistic' or is safe for human use, it doesn't automatically follow that it is either safe or appropriate for your pet.

Always follow the manufacturer's instructions, and *always* consult your vet if your dog has any health problems, or is taking any medications before giving him any non-prescription or holistic remedies aimed at helping him to cope with Firework Night. Many holistic remedies are not only potentially powerful in their effect, but require in-depth knowledge and experience in order to achieve the greatest measure of success, so in our opinion it is safest as well as likely to be most effective if you consult a qualified practitioner in the modality you are interested in trying, should you decide to pursue this course.

Another argument in favour of seeking expert advice is that while many holistic remedies work well and safely when used in combination with each other, there are exceptions. Essential oils for example, will lessen the effect of homeopathic remedies, some may not be safe to use where certain health conditions are present, and some can also be dermal irritants or photoreactive.

HERBAL REMEDIES

Herbalism is one of the most ancient forms of medicine; an appropriate herbal remedy can help to take the edge off an anxiety so may be beneficial when used to complement modalities such as Tellington TTouch or during desensitization programmes.

Nowadays you will find plenty of commercial herbal preparations available online and stocked in pet stores, which aim to reduce anxiety. Herbal remedies should however, always be treated with great respect and used with care; we suggest that for your pet's welfare you always err on the side of caution and consult a vet knowledgeable in the use of herbs. Do bear in mind that just because a product is advertised as being 'natural' or 'traditional' it doesn't mean that it is either safe or suitable for your dog. Some may be harmful to use where certain health issues are present, and they should never be given alongside conventional drugs except under the advice of a veterinary surgeon with appropriate knowledge and experience in this area, in case they conflict with the medication or even combine with it to produce toxic doses. Care should also be exercised in using herbal preparations in conjunction with homeopathy or Applied Zoopharmacognosy.

Do not give your dog herbal preparations formulated for humans except under veterinary advice, as what is good for people isn't always good for dogs. Even where a product is labelled as being specifically for dogs, do still check and research all the ingredients and once again, consult with a vet if you have any concerns. Many of the 'calming' herbal remedies contain ingredients including skullcap, valerian, passion-flower, marshmallow, chamomile, lemon balm, vervain, and lime flowers, all of which are commonly considered as being relatively safe in small doses – but we have spotted some which also contain hops, the flower cones of which are generally regarded as being toxic to dogs. Even those herbs deemed to be 'relatively safe' are not necessarily appropriate for all dogs: valerian for example, may be unsuitable for dogs who are pregnant or suffering from liver disease, and shouldn't be given prior to surgical procedures requiring anaesthesia.

It is essential only to purchase products from reputable, established companies who exercise good quality control procedures to ensure that no contamination or misidentification of the ingredients occurs. Dosage guidelines should be very carefully followed – more is not better, and can often be harmful if given in excess; there may also be cumulative effects with some herbs, making them unsuitable for long term use.

Some herbs will need time to build up effectiveness, so it may be necessary to start giving them well in advance of the time you expect to hear the first fireworks. Some dogs may also experience the opposite of the desired effect and become more hyperactive or anxious: Toni knows of a number of dogs who became worse, rather than better, after an herbal remedy was given.

HOMEOPATHY

Because homeopathy addresses the whole body, it can be as successful in helping with emotional issues as with physical problems. Pioneered and developed by Samuel Hahnemann in the eighteenth century, it is based on the principle that 'like cures like' following his discovery that substances which produced the same symptoms as an ailment, could, when given in much smaller quantities, cure it. These substances are diluted in a special process known as potentisation, and subjected to succussion (vigorous shaking) which increases the homeopathic strength even though the chemical concentration decreases.

Homeopathy is a very safe modality, and if the wrong remedy is chosen, it will simply have no effect and do no harm. Homeopathic remedies are obtainable from chemists, health shops and online, where they are most commonly supplied as 6c or 30c 'potencies'. This refers to the dilution and succussion of the remedy – the higher the number the more times it has undergone this process and the more powerful the effect may be.

Homeopathic remedies come in either liquid, tablet, pill or crystal form and need to be stored and administered correctly: the general advice is that they should not be given with food, or close to mealtimes, and should be stored away from strong smells and direct sunlight. Avoid handling them as this can also destroy their efficacy. Keep them in their original container, and if you drop a pill on the floor, discard it.

As the remedies aren't unpleasant tasting there isn't usually a problem with giving them, although you can if necessary crush tablets or pills between two spoons, place into a fold of paper and tip them into your dog's mouth so they stick to his tongue. Liquid remedies can sometimes be easier to manage - you will know your dog and which form will be the simplest to give.

Allow fifteen minutes before or after eating, and at

least five minutes between remedies if you are giving more than one. Simply tip into the bottle cap if giving pills or crystals (some bottes have a handy dispenser system that releases single pills into the cap), open your dog's mouth, and tip in. With liquids, place a few drops on to your dog's tongue or lips. Do not let the cap come into contact with your dog's mouth. If you do find any difficulties in dosing, try adding ten drops of a liquid remedy to his water bowl - but remember just how acute a dog's senses are, and check that he continues to happily drink from that bowl.

Remedies commonly suggested for fearfulness of fireworks include:

Aconite: Very fearful, terror stricken, staring eyes, panting, trembling, pacing and circling: responds rapidly and violently to noises.

Argent. Nit: Jumpy, anxious, restless, often trembling, loose bowels, nervous apprehension.

Phosphorus: Easily startled by any noise and may leap suddenly if you drop something, often thirsty, dislikes being on own and prefers to be in company, desires comfort and reassurance.

Gelsemium: Abject fear, trembling, shaking, may be rooted to the spot with fear, involuntary urination, may want to hide away.

It will do no harm to try any of these remedies; if they are not the right ones for your dog then they will simply have no effect. The success of homeopathy does rely on closely matching the right remedy (or remedies) to the individual, taking into account not only physical symptoms but background, lifestyle, environment, demeanour, character, likes, dislikes, fears, diet, household and family details and responses to various external influences. If the remedies you have chosen are not working, or only at a very superficial level it may be that the potency or frequency of dosing needs to be changed, or that an entirely different remedy will be more appropriate: seek professional help from a homeopathic veterinary practitioner.

APPLIED ZOOPHARMACOGNOSY

Essential oils and floral sprays (plant essences in a more diluted form, also called aromatic waters – not to be confused with Bach and other flower essences), can be a powerful and effective way of helping to calm your pet, and if correctly selected and administered can be amazingly helpful.

Applied Zoopharmacognosy is not quite the same as aromatherapy, which you may be familiar with in a human context: an AZ practitioner is more akin to an herbalist who possesses an in-depth knowledge of pharmacokinetics than an Aromatherapist. The essential oils are used differently with animals, employing a process of 'self-selection' whereby the most suitable oil or oils are selected by allowing your dog to do the actual choosing himself. This is done by offering him in turn those which you think are likely to be the most helpful. This is done slowly, with the open bottle held approximately 30 cm to one metre away from his nose, and his reaction to each carefully observed. Treatment should ideally be started at least ten days before you expect to hear the first fireworks. The appropriate oil can be determined before you actually expect to hear any loud noises, since even though it may be quiet and your dog not exhibiting any signs of anxiety at that particular moment in time, the problem still exists. It is crucial that only high quality oils, prepared especially for this purpose are used - those intended for use in burners are not suitable.

Oils should never be enforced on your dog with burners and diffusers, or applied to his body, unless he clearly indicates that he wants this. If you wish to use a burner or diffuser in your home for your own benefit, then do leave a door open so that your dog can move to another room if he wishes.

Offering oils

Before offering any oils to your dog, take the time to create a good working environment. In a multi-pet household, other animals should be shut away while working with the oils, and your dog should have the option available at all times of leaving the room you are both in. Prop the door open and leave him off the leash so he is always free to move away if he wishes. It is also nice to have a comfortable dog bed in the room so that if he wants to, he can lie down while working with the oils; ensure that a bowl of drinking water is also available. Oils should be offered at a time when your dog has few distractions; not, for example, near to the time when he is usually fed or when he is anticipating going for a walk. Plenty of time should be set aside, as some dogs may want to work with the oils for an extended period, especially the first time they are offered.

Different dogs may choose different oils for a similar issue; some may choose more than one, and they may also need the oils to be offered in a specific order, so finding the right oils can be a very individual matter. Upon being offered the oils, your dog's responses need to be carefully noted and correctly interpreted.

The process of narrowing down and then fine-tuning the most appropriate oil or oils is not always a simple procedure. Knowledge of the actions of the oils is essential: they can be *very* potent, and some may not be appropriate to use where certain health conditions are present or if your dog is pregnant or receiving any medication. They may also lessen or extinguish completely the effect of any homeopathic remedies that are being given.

If you wish to explore this fascinating modality, we would therefore suggest that you first read Caroline Ingraham's informative book *Help Your Dog Heal Itself,* which explains the whole process in depth, together with details of a number of oils. Alternatively, you might find it helpful to arrange a consultation with an AZ practitioner, who will have a wide range of oils your dog can select from, which can save you a lot of unnecessary expense. Do check that the practitioner is up-to-date in their knowledge; a register is currently being compiled – see the Contacts and Resources section for further details.

One final note: what your dog needs may not be what *you* need. You may have adverse reactions to certain oils, such as disliking the smell, or finding that it makes you feel sleepy or unwell.

PET REMEDY

A product called Pet Remedy is widely available in pet shops and online as either a spray, diffuser or battery operated atomiser and many owners have reported beneficial effects. The manufacturer's information describes it as a low dosage Valerian blend (it also contains Vetiver, Sweet Basil and Sage) but because it is based on essential oils, we would suggest that you observe the same general guidelines as for Applied Zoopharmacognosy: first see if your dog likes the smell, by offering him the option of sniffing at the spray applied to your hand or a tissue, or if using the diffuser, leaving a door open so that he can either stay or leave the room if he wishes. If he appears to be happy about it, the diffuser, introduced a week in advance of any expected fireworks is probably the best option.

The manufacturers state that although Pet Remedy is gentle in its effect and safe to use in most situations, if your pet is on any medications you should consult your vet before using it.

FLOWER REMEDIES

Flower essences (not to be confused with aromatic floral sprays) can be helpful with a wide range of issues: they are also available as combinations especially formulated for use in acute emergency situations, such as accidents, shock or distress of any sort. Probably the best known of these is Bach Flower Rescue Remedy which can help to take the edge off anxiety while fireworks are going off or when working through a desensitization programme. It is not a sedative or tranquilizer, but acts to gently rebalance emotions and address negative states of mind. It can be used in conjunction with conventional as well as homeopathic and herbal remedies and is very safe to use: as far as we are aware, adverse effects have never been reported - but we would suggest that, as always, you err on the side of safety and check first with your vet before giving it to your pet.

Useful for general calming in emergency situations or at times of stress, Bach Flower Rescue Remedy is a combination of five different remedies: Star of Bethlehem (shock and trauma), Rock Rose (terror),

Clematis (faintness), Impatiens (agitation), and Cherry Plum (loss of control) and is useful for general calming. Other flower remedies may use similar combinations or include additional essences.

Rescue Remedy can be bought over the counter at most high street chemists and health shops as well as online – look out for the pet-friendly version which is alcohol free. Start giving four drops three or four times a day to your dog around a fortnight before Firework Night as well as on the day itself. It can be administered in a variety of different ways – but do not try and place drops directly into his mouth as this can be stressful for most dogs and runs the risk of you (or the dropper) being bitten.

The Rescue Remedy can be added to drinking water or food, or offered on pieces of dry bread or treats which will absorb the liquid; alternatively, place it on the top of the nose where your dog will reflexively lick it off. It can also be applied to the pads of the paws, or on the belly; or to the acupressure point which lies halfway between his ears by dropping the remedy onto the palm of your hand and then stroking it on top of his head. Choose whichever method causes least stress to your dog, and is easy and safe for you to do.

You can also give Rescue Remedy at any time when fireworks are being let off which you haven't been able to anticipate in advance, or during unpredictable events such as thunderstorms. If your dog's distress affects you, or you are frightened of thunder yourself, you may find it helpful to dose yourself at the same time, so you don't transmit your own anxiety to your dog.

Rescue Remedy and the other flower essence products available will be generalized rather than specific to your dog. As with homeopathy, the better the match the better the result, so you might like to make up your own blend. There are good publications which will explain more about flower essences and how to do this or you could contact a practitioner – see the Further Reading section at the end of this book.

ACUPRESSURE

Acupressure is an ancient Eastern healing art which has been used successfully on both humans and animals for at least four thousand years. It can be beneficial in helping to resolve injuries and health issues, can play a part in pain relief, and in generally maintaining good health and vitality. It can also trigger the release of feel-good hormones, promoting relaxation and transforming habitual stress responses into calmer feelings.

A core belief of acupressure is that an intangible energetic component called 'chi', which is responsible for life and health, circulates throughout the whole of the body along invisible but very real pathways called meridians. If a chi energy disruption happens for some reason, it can cause a blockage (or 'stagnation') along the meridian and an imbalance can occur, which can lead to physical and psychological health issues.

Acupuncture and acupressure are both ways of clearing such blockages and enabling the harmonious flow of chi to be restored; this is achieved through stimulation of specific 'acupoints' which are located along the meridians where they run close to the surface of the body. Acupuncture employs the use of very fine needles which are quickly inserted, while acupressure relies on the use of the hands and fingers instead to apply pressure to the acupoints. Both techniques work very effectively, but only a qualified vet can perform an acupuncture treatment.

Applying acupressure:

Use whichever Point Work technique is most comfortable for you and your dog. In general, the two-finger technique seems to be particularly good for smaller dogs and for the extremities on larger dogs, while the thumb technique works well for larger dogs.

(image courtesy of Tallgrass Animal Acupressure Institute)

Direct thumb technique:

Gently place the tip of your thumb directly on the acupressure point at a 45-90 degree angle adding a little pressure (see picture above).

Two-finger technique:

Put your middle finger on top of your index finger and then place your index finger at a 45-90 degree angle gently, but with intentional firmness, directly on the acupressure point (see picture below).

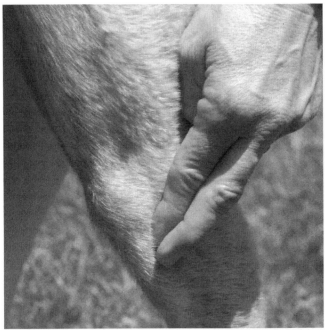

(image courtesy of Tallgrass Animal Acupressure Institute)

Accurately locating the acupoints does require a degree of anatomical knowledge, and there is potential for causing discomfort to your dog if you are incorrect or over-enthusiastic in your technique, so if you are at all uncertain in your abilities we suggest that rather than applying direct pressure you instead simply try gently rubbing or scratching with your fingers, which will still produce beneficial effects.

If you would like to find out more and learn how to confidently apply a more direct acupressure technique, we recommend attending a course or arranging for some instruction from a qualified animal acupressure practitioner: there is also an excellent book on the subject (see Further Reading and Contacts & Resources). Alternatively, you could arrange for a qualified practitioner to give your dog an acupuncture or acupressure treatment.

When working on your dog, please observe the same guidelines as those detailed in the section on Tellington TTouch, and do not enforce contact on your pet if he is concerned about you touching any areas of his body. This may indicate the presence of a health issue and you should ask your vet to investigate further. Acupressure should not be used if your dog is pregnant, and consult your vet or a qualified veterinary acupuncturist if your dog is on medication for any health conditions.

Starting a session
Find a warm, quiet and comfortable place for you and your dog, and have the chart of acupoints ready to refer to.

Start by gently placing one hand on his shoulder. With the other one, following the Bladder Meridian chart (overleaf) stroke smoothly and gently along and down his neck and along his body, staying to the side of the spine, then down the hindquarters and along the outside of the hind leg. It doesn't matter if your dog is sitting, standing or lying down, as long as he is comfortable and feels safe.

Note any areas he may be reluctant for you to touch or which he twitches when you run your hand over them. Repeat this procedure three times on each side.

We'd suggest only working a few acupoints each time, and only spending 5-15 seconds on each one. Some points may be sore for your dog so work *very* carefully, observing his body language at all times. The area may spasm when you touch it, or your dog may move away or try to nudge your hand away from the area. If your dog objects to what you are doing, stop and seek the help of a qualified vet or acupressure practitioner. Your intentions may be good but if wrongly applied may cause discomfort, pain and distress to your dog as well as putting yourself at risk.

Bladder Meridian

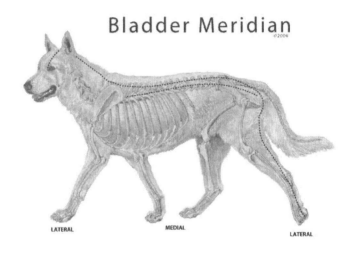

LATERAL   MEDIAL   LATERAL

(image courtesy of Tallgrass Animal Acupressure Institute)

Acupressure Session to Reduce Fear & Anxiety

• **Large Intestine 4 (LI 4)** by regulating chi within the body, LI 4 can reduce body tension in general which is helpful in bringing down the dog's stress level.

• **Heart 7 (Ht 7)** is the go-to acupoint for calming the spirit of the dog. It is a powerful point for clearing fear and anxiety at any time and especially when facing a particularly scary experience.

• **Pericardium 6 (Pe 6)** – Though Pe 6 is known for

digestive issues, it also used extensively for calming the mind and relieving anxiety.

● **Bai Hui** - Located on the midline of the sacrum where you can't feel the spinous processes. This point is traditionally called 'Heavens Gate' - most dogs love being scratched there! It generates energy along the spine, and is also a calming point which produces a feeling of wellbeing and is helpful with apprehensive, worried dogs.

Acupressure Session to Reduce Fear & Anxiety

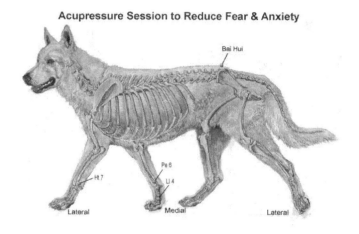

Points	Location
LI 4	At the dewclaw, medial aspect of the foreleg.
Ht 7	Located on the outside of the foreleg, in the deep crease of the carpal joint.
Pe 6	Located on the inside of the foreleg, about 2 inches above the carpal (wrist).
Bai Hui	Found on dorsal midline at the lumbosacral space.

When to work the points:

You can work the points daily, and an hour before you anticipate hearing any fireworks. Start with the highest point, and work from top to bottom, front to back and on both sides of the body.

DESENSITIZATION

This is a process which aims to help your dog overcome his fears by exposing him on a daily basis to
sound recordings of firework noises in a carefully
controlled way. It is a long term option which requires commitment and will work best if you can fit
in several sessions a week, and the whole process
must be managed with extreme care to avoid trauma-
tizing your dog even further. Although desensitization
can be very successful in resolving moderate fears and
phobias, some may be resistant to behaviour modification. Recordings can never replicate the air movement created by fireworks, so although you may be
able to accustom them to the sounds, they may still
exhibit a degree of anxiety. It is absolutely essential
to avoid creating fear during the procedure or your
dog will become worse and it will be harder to help
him, so if you see any worsening of his reactions, stop
and seek professional help.

Good quality recordings and sound systems are
needed in order to create the most realistic possible
reproduction of the firework noises. The recordings
are initially played at the very lowest possible volume
while normal family life goes on as usual, and they can
also be played during enjoyable activities such as eating or playing, or while working around a Confidence
Course (see the section on Tellington TTouch for
more information).

The noise may be barely audible to you, but remember that your dog's hearing is much keener than
yours. If your dog is very noise sensitive, you may
even need to play the recordings in a different room

to the one he is in. Very, very gradually, and only as he accepts the noises, the volume can be increased a little at a time. You may find that using a Thunder-shirt and/or utilising modalities such as homeopathy, Bach Flower Rescue Remedy, Adaptil, Pet Remedy, Applied Zoopharmacognosy and Tellington TTouch will help your dog to be calmer and more relaxed while working on the desensitization process. In very extreme cases, it may be necessary, with veterinary guidance, to use medication to support your dog through the process.

Setting up the speakers in different positions each time you play the recordings will ensure that your dog doesn't associate the noises as always coming from the same place, because real fireworks won't either! Similarly, vary the recordings you use. When he has reached the stage where he is coping well with the recordings being played fairly loudly in one location, you can begin introducing them in other areas of the house too. Each time you move to a different place, always start again at the first step, with the very lowest volume possible.

It is vital not to rush things – the most common mistake made is to turn the volume up too loudly or trying to progress too fast. Desensitization is a slow process, and one which depending on the level of concern, may take months rather than weeks for some dogs. It is important that you observe your dog very carefully to help you decide when he is ready for each new step and it is best to err on the side of caution, especially during the early sessions. You will find Turid Rugaas' book *On Talking Terms with Dogs*, Sarah Fisher's book *Unlock Your Dog's Potential* and Toni's own book *The Truth about Wolves and Dogs* invaluable in helping you to develop your observational skills and to correctly interpret your dog's body language. If you lack experience in this area, it may be advisable, both for success and your own safety, to seek guidance from a professional. Always remember that a dog which is feeling stressed may behave out of character and could be inclined to snap.

ADAPTIL

Adaptil (formerly known as DAP) is a synthetic copy of a natural canine pheromone produced by nursing bitches which helps to comfort and reassure their puppies. It can also help adult dogs, promoting calmness and reducing anxiety during times of stress. It is colourless and odourless, with no sedative effect and can be safely used alongside medications. Although it doesn't work with all dogs, it can be very effective for many, helping them feel safe and secure.

It is available from vets, pet shops and online as a collar, a reusable diffuser (similar to air freshener devices) and as a spray. The diffuser is plugged into an electrical socket and left continuously running in the room where your dog spends most time. It covers up to 50-70 square metres, and although fully functional after 24 hours, for best results it should ideally be started a fortnight before any fireworks are expected. The diffuser will last for around 4 weeks, and is reusable – refill vials can be bought and replaced as needed.

The action of the diffuser can be further reinforced on nights that fireworks are heard by applying the Adaptil spray to the den or bedding. Allow 15 minutes between spraying any objects and allowing the dog to use them: its effect will last for around 2-3 hours.

TELLINGTON TTOUCH METHOD

Because we have both owned dogs with noise
phobias, we know only too well just how distressing
occasions like Fireworks Night can be for pets. Along
with many others, we have found the Tellington
TTouch Method to be one of the most successful and
effective ways of helping our pets to cope with and
overcome their fear of fireworks and other loud noises. TTouch is easy to learn, can be done yourself in
the comfort of your own home, and needs no special
skills or knowledge of anatomy. Ideally you should
put in some pre-season preparation, but even if out-
of-season fireworks going off catch you unprepared, a
few minutes of TTouch can make a world of difference.

Just how phenomenally successful Tellington
TTouch can be is illustrated by Toni's own experiences with her dog, Buzz. While training to become a
Tellington TTouch Companion Animal Practitioner,
Toni practised what she was learning on Buzz and
having been told that the TTouch work could help
with noise phobia, she increased the amount of work
she did with him during the approach of the fireworks season and put him in a body wrap each evening.

Previously Buzz would hide under the table, pant,
dig and be very distressed, and even after all the
noises had stopped, Toni would be unable to
persuade him to go outside to relieve himself until the
next morning. After introducing TTouch she noticed
a dramatic shift in his behaviour: he could lie asleep
next to her, and should a particularly loud bang go off

and wake him she could quickly calm him with a few minutes of the TTouch body work. He also became willing to go out in the garden for a last pee before bedtime. Successive years saw even more improvement, and when Toni got caught out on one occasion, Buzz happily sniffed around while fireworks were going off overhead.

If you have recently acquired a new dog, we'd both recommend that you don't wait for problems to begin (or to discover whether one exists), but to be proactive so it doesn't occur in the first place. This was exactly what Toni did with her next dog, Bea. Instead of waiting to find out how she felt about fireworks, Toni worked with her daily on the lead-up to her first firework season, and on the night itself she was calm and happy. It also put her in good stead for coping with thunder, crop scarers and gunshots: she never had any problems with them - not bad for a dog who was so noise sensitive when she first came to live with Toni that even the whooshing of an air freshener used to startle her!

Tellington TTouch really can help dogs frightened of fireworks, as well as helping them to cope with other stressful events and situations. Many dogs show improvement after receiving TTouch work and most go on to grow in confidence each year if it is continued, with the degree of anxiety not only diminishing to more bearable levels but often vanishing altogether.

About Tellington TTouch
Devised nearly forty years ago by Linda Tellington Jones, and developed in conjunction with her sister Robyn Hood, Tellington TTouch is often confused

with massage. It is actually very different, and as well as the special 'TTouches' employs a varied system of exercises which include groundwork and body wraps.

The Tellington TTouch Method – or TTouch® (pronounced Tee Touch) for short – has a proven track record for helping animals with a wide range of issues, including noise phobias. A kind, non-invasive, generally well accepted and empathic way of working with animals, it is easy to learn, simple to apply, and gives you a vital role at a time when you may have previously felt helpless and frustrated.

The Tellington TTouch Method is based on the principle that posture and behaviour are inextricably linked, with posture affecting behaviour and vice versa. By improving posture, balance and movement, beneficial physical, psychological and emotional changes are produced, with self-confidence and self-control increasing. Mind and body begin to work together in harmony and unwanted behaviours diminish or disappear entirely. This is not some far-fetched or whimsical theory, but one which has been successfully demonstrated time and time again, both with Tellington TTouch and in other modalities which focus on posture, such as Alexander Technique.

The work can be done with your dog in preparation for the firework season and can also be used when he is fearful without danger of reinforcing the negative behaviour.

Your dog will not be the only one to benefit from the work. Although you may not be worried about loud noises yourself, you may be concerned on his behalf. This can lead to you sending out anxiety signals which your dog may pick up on, causing him to become even more worried. How many of us, when hearing a bang, will stop, hold our breath and look at our dogs to check their reaction? Without intending to, you will have just performed three actions that tell your dog there is something to be worried about. Because Tellington Touch enables you to be proactive, it can help you to feel more in control of the situation and therefore to be more composed.

TTouch provides you with the tools to make changes for the better for your fearful dog – but if you own other pets which don't have any issues in need of resolution, it is still worth spending a little time performing a few of the TTouches on them too, as it is a wonderfully enjoyable way of creating and deepening bonds of trust and affection between you.

'Reading' your dog

It is often forgotten just how closely connected posture and behaviour are, even though we constantly use phrases such as having cold feet, gritting our teeth, or tearing our hair out to describe states of mind. We can also perceive how someone is feeling by observing their posture: a happy person will literally be 'standing tall', walking with a bounce in their step, head up and quite possibly a smile on their face. Conversely a depressed person will appear to be drooping, hunched up, with rounded shoulders and a slower, dragging stride.

Just as body language can reflect a state of mind, so the reverse can be true, with poor posture or the presence of 'tension patterns' directly influencing the mental and emotional processes and dictating behaviour.

Dogs with physical and/or behavioural issues frequently exhibit tension patterns. These can develop for a variety of reasons, including physical injury, health issues, frightening experiences and emotional trauma. The tension produced and sustained in specific areas of the body promotes different responses; for example, a dog which holds tension through his hind quarters will often tend to be fearful – these individuals also often suffer from noise sensitivity.

Tension patterns show up in many ways. There may be a very hot or cold area on the body: the skin may feel stiff and immobile rather than sliding freely across the underlying tissues: changes in coat colour or texture may be seen, or greasy or dry scurfy patches: swirls and changes of direction in the way the hairs grow may be noticed. Muscling and wear and tear on the nails and pads may differ from one side to the other ... It is a fascinating study, and as you learn to look at your dog in more detail, you will learn a lot about him which can make it easier to help him. More detailed information on tension patterns and how to identify them can be found in Sarah Fisher's book *Unlock Your Dog's Potential* (see Further Reading).

Observing your dog is an important part of TTouch work, but it will also benefit you in all other areas of your relationship; noting your dog's posture, how he moves and responds to his environment and the situations he finds himself in will tell you a lot about how he is feeling physically and provide an invaluable key to his mental processes and emotional state.

Learning to 'read' your dog's posture will help you to decide which TTouches to use and where to use them: when to start, and when to stop: and help ensure that you stay safe. You may need to exercise care when handling or performing TTouches on areas which hold a lot of tension as your dog may be reluctant for you to touch him there, and it may even cause him discomfort when you do. Always keep this latter point in mind, and do read carefully through the section on safety.

Tellington TTouch Body Work: The TTouches

The advice commonly given to owners is to ignore their pet when he is exhibiting signs of fear, but as you probably already know, for a concerned owner this can be a very tough strategy to try and follow, and one that can cause your own stress levels to rise too, exacerbating matters. Tellington TTouch on the other hand, actively encourages a hands-on approach; a course of action which most owners prefer and find much easier to adopt. Contrary to the frequently recommended advice of following a policy of non-interaction with your dog, TTouch will **not** reinforce your dog's fears.

The special 'TTouches' involve gently moving the skin in various ways. They are the foundation of the Tellington TTouch Method and provide a positive way of calming and reassuring, helping your dog to relax, releasing tension and lowering his stress levels. Anyone can do them, no specialised knowledge of anatomy is needed, and they can be used either on their own, in conjunction with other modalities or with Tellington TTouch equipment such as body wraps (explained further on).

You can learn how to do the TTouches by reading a book, watching a video, attending a workshop or demo or asking a practitioner to visit (details in the Contacts & Resources section), and once the basic skills are learnt you can apply them anywhere, anytime, whenever your pet has need of them. It takes only a short time to learn how to produce a beneficial effect, although the more you practise, the better you will become at it.

The TTouches should be introduced before Firework Night so they are something which is already familiar, pleasurable and reassuring to your dog, and which you are confident and at ease about doing. During the run up to Firework Night try and do a little work with your dog every evening so that it is a normal part of your routine, and then if any bangs start a few days earlier, you won't be caught out.

On the day itself, have an earlier TTouch session with your dog so that he is relaxed and in a calm state of mind. This state of calm will be aided by wearing a body wrap. When the fireworks do begin you can follow up this earlier session with a bit more TTouch body work if you see him becoming upset. If your dog is lying down quietly however, leave him alone and don't disturb him.

How to introduce TTouch Bodywork
While doing the TTouches be sure not to lean over your dog, as this might intimidate or frighten him. It is safer for you and more comfortable for your dog if you position yourself to the side of, and just behind his head, so that you are both facing in the same direction. This will enable you to see him and to monitor his responses clearly but without staring directly at him which he may find confrontational. It also makes it easy for him to move away if he wishes, without having to go through you in order to do so.

Bear in mind that if your dog's stress affects you – which it may do even if you aren't directly aware of it – it can be easy to start doing the TTouches rather fast. This can then have the opposite effect to the one you are trying to produce: generally, doing the TTouches slowly is calming while going faster tends to be stimulating.

Be sensitive to indications from your dog that he has had enough and needs a break. You will find that lots of short sessions often work better than one long one, and can easily be fitted into odd moments during the day when you have a few minutes to spare. We suggest that the longest you work with your dog should be no more than around twenty minutes, and incorporating a few mini-breaks into the session if needed. Signs that your dog may need a break include him looking unsettled, moving away from you, becoming distracted, and fidgeting. Stop for a while and allow your dog to reposition himself. If he readily settles down for some more work, continue, but if he responds again in a similar way, then it is probably time to end the session and try again another time. Very often you will find that what may have been difficult for your dog to cope with today, may be easier for him tomorrow. Give your dog the benefit of the doubt, keep sessions short and listen to him.

Before you start!

Before you get started on using the TTouches, for maximum benefit and to avoid inadvertently stressing your dog or compromising your safety, remember the following golden rules:

▶ **If your dog wishes to move away** while doing the TTouches, allow him to do so.

▶ **Let him choose his position:** do not insist that

he stands if he feels more comfortable sitting or lying down.

▶ **Practice doing each of the TTouches on your own arms** or on a partner or friend's arms or back before trying them on your pet. This will help you to appreciate just how light and subtle you can be. Another human can also give you feedback on how it feels and help you to improve.

▶ **Concentrating on what you are doing** can sometimes make you stiff and tense, which will make the TTouches feel unpleasant to the recipient. Try to relax and keep your breathing deep and regular. Allowing your dog to hear you breathe deeply and *slowly* will also encourage him to match his rate of breathing to yours, aiding calmness.

▶ **Just the weight of your hand is enough to move the skin** while performing each of the TTouches, and you can make the contact even lighter still if your dog appears wary of the work. At no time should you press into the body; you are only working with the skin.

▶ **Make each of your TTouches as slow as possible.**

▶ **Constantly observe your dog's body language,** as this can indicate his state of mind. You will find Sarah Fisher's book *Unlock Your Dog's Potential* and Turid Rugaas' book *On Talking Terms with Dogs* helpful; but unless you have a lot of experience in this area it can be easy to misinterpret responses or miss more subtle ones. You may therefore find it helpful initially to arrange a session with a Tellington TTouch practitioner who can help you develop your powers of observation.

▶ **TTouch is something** we do **with** our animals not **to** them. Break it down into smaller steps if needed, or start the work in the Confidence Course (you will find more details about this in the following pages). Better still, contact a guild certified Tellington TTouch Practitioner for help if you are having any difficulties in applying the work.

▶ **Should your dog show concern** about you touching certain parts of his body, return to a place where he is less anxious, and when he relaxes try gradually approaching the difficult area again. If there are other signs such as stiffness, or tautness or changes in temperature of the skin, or changes in the hair colour, direction and texture of the coat, it may indicate the presence of a physical problem; ask your vet to investigate further.

Staying safe

You can do TTouches all over your dog's body, but **observe him closely** as you do so. We cannot emphasise too often that the most affectionate and placid of dogs can behave unpredictably when stressed and may strike out unexpectedly if he is frightened or feels unwell. If you lack experience in reading canine body language, a Tellington TTouch practitioner will be able to help you in developing this essential skill.

As has already been explained, fear, arousal and physical conditions are usually evident in your dog's posture as tension patterns. When you gently touch those areas the skin may feel taut and the muscles hard and tight. You may even see changes in the coat texture, and the tail might be clamped down tightly between the hind legs. If you can release the tension in these places it can make a big difference, with a more relaxed posture producing a correspondingly calmer and more relaxed state of mind: but using the TTouches to help achieve this needs to be managed with great tact and subtlety as your dog may be particularly sensitive to contact in these areas at first.

Be very gentle and watch him carefully at all times, adapting your actions according to whether they indicate a decreasing or increasing level of concern. You will find reading Turid Rugaas' book *On Talking Terms With Dogs*, and Sarah Fisher's book *Unlock Your Dog's Potential* which contains detailed information on tension patterns, invaluable guides in helping to develop your observational skills and in interpreting what you see.

If he shows a low level of concern, try using a sheepskin mitten, balled up sock or sponge to do the TTouches with. Remember to be very gentle: and in any places where a lot of tension is present making the skin and muscles very tight, it is especially essential to be light, slow and soft in your movements, so you don't cause discomfort. Doing just one or two TTouches and then pausing can also help the work to be more acceptable.

The TTouches can cause many different sensations through the body which at first may feel a little weird to your dog. Bear in mind that just because he is tolerating something, it doesn't necessarily mean that he is enjoying it, so act with caution and keep observing his responses closely – although not by staring hard at him which he may find alarming!

If he is still concerned or the level of anxiety increases, don't enforce the TTouches. Work instead on a different area which your dog finds easy to cope with; the shoulder perhaps. As he begins to relax a little you may be able to gradually begin to approach and work on the challenging area, very briefly at first, slowly building it up one TTouch at a time. If you are at all unsure, don't persist but seek help from an experienced practitioner.

If your dog has an old injury be particularly careful when approaching the site of it. Even though it may have occurred a long time ago and be completely healed now, he may still be defensive about that part of his body and show anxiety about you touching it, especially when he is stressed. In some cases there may still be residual discomfort in the area even though to all outward appearances he seems to be fully recovered. He may also have a fear of the memory of pain in that area. If there is any doubt in the matter, ask your vet to check it out.

Remember!
If your dog doesn't like what you're doing, try:
using a lighter pressure:
and/or
a faster or slower speed:
and/or
using a soft-bristled paint brush, sheepskin mitten or balled-up sock to introduce the work
and/or
working on a different part of the body:
and/or

a different TTouch
and/or
stopping for a short period and letting your dog
move around and think about the experience
before trying again
and/or
making sessions shorter -
some dogs can only cope with a few minutes or
a few TTouches at a time to begin with.
Be patient, increasing the number of TTouches
and length of each session slowly
and/or
starting with TTouch ground work and
seeking the help of an experienced Tellington
TTouch practitioner

The Tellington TTouches
There are many different TTouches, which have all
been named after the animals that inspired them – it
also makes it a fun and easy way of remembering
which is which. We have included a few simple and
effective ones here that you might like to try and
which can be especially helpful with noise sensitivity.
Once you are familiar with them you may like to add
others to your repertoire. You can find out more by
reading the books listed in the Further Reading section, by attending a workshop or demonstration, or
working one-to-one with a TTouch practitioner. You
can also see the TTouches being demonstrated online
by visiting You Tube and searching for Tellington
TTouch for dogs - you will find plenty of video clips.

If you are a little unsure about reading your dog's
body language and want to check that he is comfortable with the body work, simply do one or two repeti-

tions of the TTouch you are performing and stop. Take your hands off your dog and move back a little from him. If he re-engages with you by looking in your direction, moving closer, nudging your arm or vocalising by maybe softly whining, whilst looking and moving towards you, then continue doing a few more TTouches. Check in often with him, by regularly stopping and asking for permission to continue. If however your dog moves away when you stop, let him. He may need a drink, or to 'think' about how the work feels. Often he will return and re-engage with you and you can continue but if not, don't force it. Go and do something else instead - play a game, go for a toilet break or finish the session there. Some dogs really do need the work drip fed in micro sessions so be led by your dog and give him the choice.

LLAMA TTOUCH

Llama TTouches are very soothing and calming, so are useful for dogs which are timid, nervous, or anxious about being touched on certain parts of the body.

The Llama TTouch can also be a great way to introduce the circular TTouches such as the Clouded Leopard, as it feels less intense to animals.

1.

Use the back of your fingers, or the back of your hand. Gently and slowly stroke along your dog's body going with the direction of the coat, and keeping your fingers slightly curved so they are nice and soft, rather than stiff *(pic 2)*. If he is comfortable with the contact, widen the area to include all of him including down the legs and along the jaw line. As well as being cooler, using the back of your hand to do TTouches may be less threatening and more readily accepted by some dogs. If you note any anxiety stay only briefly in that area before returning to a point (such as the shoulder) where he is more comfortable.

Pic 2: Llama TTouch *(image courtesy of Toni Shelbourne)*

2.

As your dog begins to relax and grow more confident about you making physical contact, in addition to stroking with the backs of your fingers or hand, try making circular movements as well as stroking ones. Very lightly and gently move the skin as you make each circle, rather than sliding over the coat.

Try visualising a clock face on your dog's body beneath your hand or fingers: your aim is to move the skin, going in a clockwise direction, from the point where the six is, all the way around the clock face and

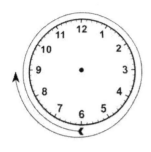

back to six again. When you reach six continue without pausing around to the nine so that you have completed one full circle plus a quarter of another one. Pause and then move to another part of the body. Ensure the skin feels as though you are lightly lifting not dragging it as you start each circle - experiment on your own arm to check.

Make each circle as slow as possible, staying soft and light and noting any signs of concern from your dog; if you do spot any, simply stop for a few moments or return to a place on his body where he is more accepting of the body work.

ZEBRA TTOUCH

This is another good TTouch to use with dogs who are overly sensitive about contact, and who may dislike being petted.

It's great for gaining the attention of a nervous and excitable dog, and for calming an anxious, noise phobic one.

1.

Position yourself to one side of your dog – he can be sitting, standing or lying down. Start with your fingers and thumb relaxed and gently curved.

Resting the hand on the top of his shoulder, slide it downwards, allowing your thumb and fingers to spread apart as it moves downwards, towards the floor or the feet of your dog.

2.

As your hand comes back up towards the spine, allow the fingers to loosely close together again. Keep the pressure light, but firm enough that you don't tickle *(pic 3).*

Pic 3: Zebra TTouch   *(image courtesy of Sarah Fisher)*

3.

Change the angle of your hand slightly each time you complete an upwards or downwards movement so that your hand travels along the length of your dog's body from shoulder to hindquarters in a zigzag pattern.

When you've finished, switch sides and repeat, unless he is lying flat on his side rather than on his chest, in which case just work on the area you can reach.

SPRINGBOK TTOUCH

Visualise the distinctive high jumps of the Springbok antelope as it leaps vertically into the air with all four legs at once, and you'll have a good idea of this TTouch which is named after it. It can settle a nervous or hyperactive dog, and if he is so agitated that he cannot listen to you, the Springbok TTouch may be a way in which you can help him come back down to earth and pay attention. Once he starts to settle and focus on you, you can then switch to one of the other TTouches.

1.

Lightly place the tips of the fingers and thumb of one hand on your dog's body, with the thumb about two inches away from your fingers.

Move your fingers and thumb away off the body in a quick, light, upward, sliding motion while simultaneously bringing them together *(pic 4).*

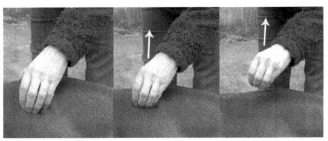

Pic 4: Springbok   *(image courtesy of Toni Shelbourne)*

2.

For maximum effect this TTouch should be performed randomly and quickly over the body, skipping from one area to another.

Be very careful to keep it feeling light, delicate and airy – do not pinch or pluck at the skin with your fingertips or pull at the coat: take special care if your dog has long hair. It can be used on all areas of the body.

CLOUDED LEOPARD TTOUCH

Because this circular TTouch helps to build trust and improve co-ordination and the ability to learn, it can be really helpful with dogs which are fearful, nervous, stressed and insecure. The Clouded Leopard TTouch can be used all over the body, even in areas such as the tail and face. Generally it is easiest to start on your dog's shoulder area and work out from there, returning to this area if need be.

1.

Position yourself to the side and slightly behind your dog. Rest one hand lightly on his body. Softly curve the fingers of your other hand, so that it looks a bit like a leopard's paw. Lightly place the pads of the fingers on your dog's body, with the thumb a little apart from them to help steady your hand. Your wrist should be straight and relaxed at all times to enable the fingers and wrist to rotate as you perform the movement.

2.

Using the pads of the finger tips, gently move your dog's skin in a clockwise circle about 1 cm in diameter. Maintain the same speed for the whole movement. It helps if you imagine that your fingers are travelling around a clock face: start each circle where the six would be and move in a clockwise direction all the way around the dial – but when you return to the six position again, keep on going to nine o'clock on the clock face so that you have completed one full circle plus a quarter of another one. Try to make your circles as slow as possible *(pic 5 overleaf).*

3.

Keep your wrist and fingers relaxed, and maintain a light but consistent pressure and speed. Do not press into your dog's skin – use no more than just the weight of your hand.

After completing each TTouch, stop, pause for a slow breath and then slide your fingers lightly across the coat to a new spot about a hands' width away and begin another circle.

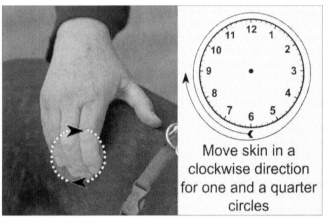

Move skin in a clockwise direction for one and a quarter circles

Pic 5: Clouded Leopard *(image courtesy of David & Charles)*

4.

Remember to start each circle at the 'six' point, with six being the point nearest to the ground. Ensure that the skin feels as though you are lightly lifting, not dragging it as you start each circle – experiment on your own arm to check.

5.

Remember that you should be moving the skin with your fingers, rather than allowing your fingers to glide over the surface. If your dog is long coated, you may find it more effective to lightly reposition your fingers into the coat slightly so you can more easily feel his skin.

6.

When working over bony areas, or places where he is concerned about being touched, make your contact with your dog's body much lighter, so you are hardly touching him at all while still moving the skin under your fingers. If the skin feels tight, do not try and force it to move, but try making the circles using a larger surface area (by using either the whole of your hand or half the length of your fingers) and continue to use the lightest of pressures and to be very slow in the movement.

7.

Working randomly over your dog's body can sometimes grab the attention of the nervous system better than 'connected' TTouches, i.e. linking them by sliding your fingers across the skin from the circle you have just completed to the place where you are going to start the next one, so that you maintain a constant light contact with him. Try lifting your hand after each circle instead and gently placing it somewhere else on your dog's body: experiment to see which works best for your dog, and bear in mind that preferences may change from day to day or even hour to hour.

8.

If your dog still appears reluctant about allowing you to work on certain areas, move back to a place where he enjoys the feel of the TTouch and dip in and out of the areas of concern as described previously. For some dogs, this TTouch may feel quite intense: if it is too much for him initially try the Llama or Zebra TTouch instead.

EAR WORK

Ear work can have a wonderfully calming, comforting and soothing effect, helping to lower stress levels and heart rate when done slowly. The majority of dogs enjoy Ear work, and most owners naturally stroke their dog's ears anyway.

1.

Position yourself so that both you and your dog are facing in the same direction. Lightly place one hand on his body. Use the back of your other hand to stroke softly along the outside edge of one ear.

2.

If your dog is happy about this, cup your hand around the ear and stroke from the base to the tip. Try to mould as much of your hand as possible around the dog's ear for maximum contact. If your dog has up-right ears work in an upwards direction: if they flop downwards, work in a horizontal outwards and downwards direction.

3.

Next, take the ear between the thumb and curved forefingers of one hand so that you only have one layer of ear flap between fingers and thumb. Slide them along the length of the ear, working from the base right out to the end or tip *(pic 6).* Move your hand slightly each time you begin a new stroke so that you cover every part of the ear. Be gentle and work slowly to help calm and relax. At the tip of the ear is an acupressure 'shock' point: make a small circle there with the tip of your forefinger to stimulate it, and then slide your fingers off. This is beneficial for dogs that are habitually nervous.

Pic 6: Earwork *(image courtesy of David & Charles)*

4.

If your dog is holding his ears in a furled, pinned or high ear carriage, very gently unfurl them as you slide along each ear, and bringing it into a more natural, relaxed position. Posture can directly affect behaviour, so if the ears are relaxed the rest of the body will tend to follow suit.

5.

The ears of some dogs may have a rather taut connection to the head and can feel very stiff and tight – especially when they are feeling stressed.

In such instances, try a few small circular Clouded Leopard TTouches (see the section on the Clouded Leopard) around the base or gently move the whole of your dog's ear in a circular motion to help release the tension. The emphasis *must* be on small and subtle movements – while you want to try and relax the ear and surrounding tense area, if you are forcible you may inadvertently cause discomfort.

Pic 7: Earwork *(image courtesy of Sarah Fisher)*

6.

If your dog appears to dislike ear work and has floppy ears, try moulding your hand over one and gently holding it against his head. Very slowly and gently move your whole hand in a circular movement, so that his head supports his ear *(pic 7).* Make the circle small so that it is a subtle movement; he may prefer it being circled in an anti-clockwise direction to a clockwise one. If he still finds this challenging try wearing a sheepskin mitten or glove to diffuse the sensation even further. You may find that this will help to   reduce any concerns he has and to become more tolerant about Ear work. If he continues to show concern, do ask your vet to check his ears, mouth and neck, as there may be an underlying physical reason for his unease.

MOUTH WORK

Mouth work can be another useful TTouch which can help considerably with fearful behaviour during the firework season.

Working around the face and on the gums can have a positive and beneficial effect on emotional and physical responses, and improves the ability to focus and learn: there is a direct connection between the area at the front of the mouth and the limbic system in the brain, which is the seat of emotional responses and also responsible for functions including adrenaline flow, long term memory and behaviour.

Mouth work is invaluable for dealing with behaviours like barking, chewing, panting and biting and as a bonus, once your dog is accustomed to it, you will have no trouble at all in checking and brushing his teeth.

It is however, best to use this particular TTouch in preparation for fireworks but **NOT** on the night itself: it could be dangerous for you to try it at a time when your dog is very stressed - never forget that a fearful dog may behave unpredictably and out of character. Do not use this TTouch if you think your dog may nip or bite: seek expert help.

1.

Position yourself so that you are to the side of your dog, behind his head and with both of you facing in the same direction. If he turns to face you stop immediately, as this may indicate that he is not comfortable with the work.

2.

Place one hand under his chin for support, but without restricting his movement, while you stroke gently along the sides of his face and muzzle with the back of the other hand.

If he is relaxed about this, use gentle Clouded Leopard TTouches to work around the jaw muscles and lips *(pic 8).*

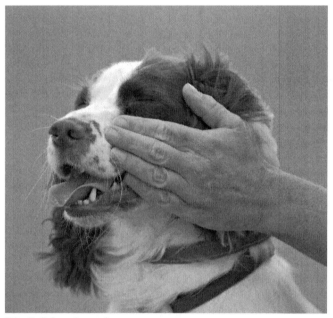

Pic 8: Mouthwork *(image courtesy of David & Charles)*

4.

When your dog is comfortable with this, quietly slip a finger or thumb under the lip and up onto the gum. Wet your finger with a little water if the mouth feels dry, so that it slides freely on the gum rather than sticking to it.

Gently run the finger around the whole gum line,

both upper and lower. Switch hands so you can work the gums on both sides of the mouth *(pic 9).* You may only be able to do this for very short periods initially.

Pic 9: Mouthwork *(image courtesy of Toni Shelbourne)*

TAIL WORK

A dog will instinctively stiffen and tuck his tail when frightened, so helping to release both the physical and emotional tension held there can be key to helping him to cope with his fears.

Although tail work can help to increase confidence in a dog which is nervous, timid and noise sensitive, do not however, assume that he will be happy for you to handle his tail or touch him around his hindquarters.

Dogs which are fearful or anxious and hold a lot of tension in these areas may find it difficult to tolerate contact there and may react defensively. Because the majority of noise sensitive dogs find this TTouch very challenging, introduce and use the work over a number of sessions and remember to dip in and out of Tail work, interspersing it with other TTouches.

If in doubt start to introduce touch to the tail with the Llama or the Clouded Leopard TTouches. You can do this while your dog is sitting so that the floor supports his tail. If he has long hair, you can also try very gently sliding small sections of hair between your fingers from the root to the tip.

As with mouth work, this TTouch may be too difficult for your dog to cope with on Firework night itself but ensure you have done plenty on the lead up to the season so that it feels loose and flexible.

1.

While your dog is standing or lying down on his side, with one hand gently take hold of the tail at its base, near his bottom. Lightly support it from underneath with your fingers, and with your thumb lying on top, the tip of it facing towards your dog's head *(pic 10)*. Lightly place your other hand on your dog's hind-quarters or under the thigh.

2.

Move the tail slowly and gently in both clockwise and then anti-clockwise directions, making sure that you keep within a comfortable range of movement. These movements need to be tiny and it can be very easy to over-exaggerate them, so it is a good idea to practise on your own fingers first to see just how little movement is needed to create an effect, and then to apply the same gentle and subtle rotation to your dog's tail.

At first the tail may feel rather wooden and hard to move: work on it for very short periods if your dog shows reluctance for you to touch him in this area; be very tactful and gentle. After a while you should notice that the range of movement gradually increases and that your dog becomes happier to have you perform this TTouch. This can take time and several sessions for some dogs.

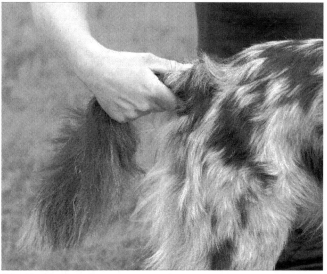

Pic 10: Tailwork *(image courtesy of David & Charles)*

3.

If your dog is very nervous, or clamps his tail down, don't try and pull it out but instead cup the palm of your hand over the top of his tail where it joins his body and gently make small clockwise and anticlockwise circular movements *(pic 11).* From this you can progress to gently holding your dog's tail against one of his own hind legs and then, starting from the base, using the whole of your hand do circular TTouches along its length all the way down to the tip. Complete each circle with a pause before sliding a little further down the tail and repeating. Fit in as many circles as you can.

Pic 11: Tailwork *(image courtesy of David & Charles)*

4.

As well as circling the tail, you can also perform a 'pearling' action along the whole length of the tail: slide your hand along the tail, from base to tip, with your fingers in the same position as in step 1. Each time you feel a vertebra, gently rock it in a downward and inwards movement towards the dog's body. This must be done very, very gently, without exaggerating the movement and while paying very close attention to your dog's response. Again, you can practice this on your own finger before trying it on your dog.

5.

No tail? No problem – even if your dog's tail is docked, you can still gently work the stump using the circular rotations or by doing Clouded Leopard TTouches along its length *(pic 12)*

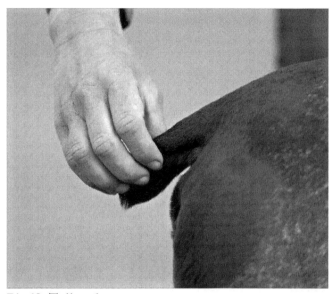

Pic 12: Tailwork   *(image courtesy of David & Charles)*

TELLINGTON TTOUCH BODY WRAPS

In addition to the special TTouches, the Tellington TTouch Method makes use of many different training aids. One of the most recognizable of these are the body wraps; employing stretchy bandages, these can be very successful with dogs that suffer from noise sensitivity as well as with issues such as separation and travel anxiety. They influence the tactile part of the sensory system and can help dogs to settle and calm. Similarly, many people with autism find that gentle pressure helps to relieve feelings of anxiety. Think of it as being a portable hug if you like - but whatever the reason why it works, the constant gentle pressure does appear to have a calming effect on the nervous system, providing reassurance and comfort if your dog is fearful or hyperactive. Fearful dogs no longer feel reliant on their owners or another canine companion as emotional props but begin to feel able to self-soothe and may become less clingy as a result.

It is important that the bandage you use is stretchy, as this allows it to provide a light pressure which stays in constant contact with your dog's body as he moves, without restricting his movement. ACE wraps are ideal and come in a range of lengths and widths according to the size of your dog: if you have difficulty getting hold of them, they can be purchased from the TTEAM office (see the Contacts & Resources section). Alternatives include horse tail or exercise bandages sold in equestrian stores, or a crepe bandage if you can't get hold of anything else. Do not use Vetrap, as it is hard to undo quickly if necessary, and the hairs of long-coated dogs can get caught up in it. Make sure there is plenty of give in the fabric; with time and use the stretchiness will eventually become lost and the wrap will need replacing.

Your dog should be introduced to wearing a wrap at least a couple of weeks before you expect to hear any fireworks so that he is accustomed to, and has positive associations with it. Provided you introduce it properly, most dogs enjoy wearing a wrap, but even if you think your pet looks a bit comical in it, don't laugh at him! Dogs can be just as sensitive as people about being ridiculed.

Ideally, use the wrap on a daily basis during the run-up to Firework Night. On the night itself, put it on before the first bangs are expected, and leave it on until after they have finished. Of course, if you get caught out by unexpected out-of-season fireworks you can still put it on as soon as you become aware of them, and should find – assuming your dog is already familiar with wearing it – that it will still work very effectively.

If you find that a wrap doesn't seem to help much on the first occasion that you use it, do persevere and remember that the key element is to use the wrap in conjunction with the TTouches. Even if you find that using a wrap or Thundershirt (see next section) used by itself helps a lot, it is still worthwhile also doing some TTouches, as this often enhances the effect even further, helping your dog to make positive, permanent changes.

Both TTouches and Body Wraps have a cumulative effect, so use them regularly. You will often find that your dog's recovery rate is the first thing to change and diminish before the actual behaviour shifts so even if it appears not to 'work' the first time, keep at it!

The Half Wrap

As we have already mentioned, wraps can be very versatile; they can be used in a variety of different configurations to help in resolving a wide number of issues. You can find out more about these in '*All Wrapped Up For Pets: Improving function, performance and behaviour with Tellington TTouch Body Wraps*' by Robyn Hood (see Further Reading). Introduce the wrap in familiar surroundings where your dog feels safe and relaxed. Initially you should start with a simple half wrap - you may find that for many dogs this is quite sufficient anyway.

1.

Approach your dog calmly with the wrap; with it bundled up in your hand, let him sniff at and take a good look at it. Stroke it gently against his sides and chest. You can even use it to do some circular TTouches on his shoulders and chest. If he is anxious about approaching it, place the wrap on the floor and put treats on top of it for him to eat.

2.

Once your dog is quite happy around the wrap, unroll and pass the centre of the bandage around the front of his chest. Bring the ends across the shoulders, up over his back and cross them over just above his shoulder blades *(pic 13).*

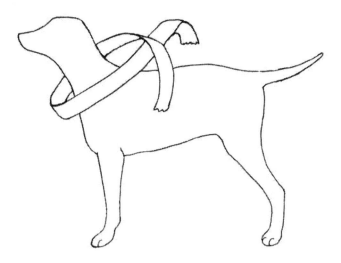

Pic 13: Putting on a half wrap

3.

Take the loose ends down the sides of his ribcage, behind the front legs. Cross them beneath his rib cage and bring them back up again over the top of his back. As you do this, keep the wrap close to his body and unravel it a little at a time from your hands so it doesn't flap around. Be careful not to inadvertently pull the ends too much at this stage, as some dogs may find this difficult to cope with. Try to be slow and smooth in your movements.

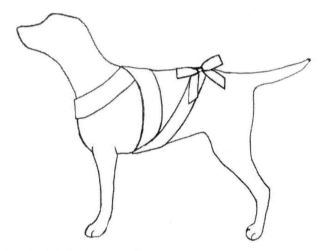

Pic 14: Finishing a half wrap

4.

Tie the ends in a bow or quick release knot so it can be quickly undone again if necessary. Make sure that the fastening lies off to one side of the spine, not directly on top of it *(pic 14)*. Alternatively, you can now buy Ace wraps with Velcro on the ends: or sew some onto the bandage you are using to secure it. The wrap should be applied just firmly enough to keep it in place and enable it to maintain contact with the body – about the same sort of pressure as an elasticated tracksuit waistband *(pic 15).* Check in various places to see if you can easily slide your hand beneath it. If it is too tight in one area and too loose in another, readjust it until the tension is the same throughout. Remember that its purpose is to provide feelings of security and sensory input, not to support and certainly shouldn't restrict movement or cause discomfort.

5.

Encourage your dog to move while wearing the wrap: if he freezes use gentle coaxing, offer a really tasty treat or invite a ***gentle*** game with a favourite toy to overcome his reluctance. Don't play wildly exciting games with him while he is wearing the wrap though, as this will elevate adrenalin levels, cancelling out its calming effect. If he rubs or grabs at it, try to distract him. If after a few minutes he is still worrying at it, remove it and do more TTouches on him by way of preparation for wearing it. Try again on another day.

6.

Even if your dog seems comfortable the first time he wears a wrap, remove it after a few minutes, and over the next few sessions gradually increase the duration it is worn for. On the build up to Fireworks Night keep the wrap on for a maximum of around twenty minutes before removing it; on the night itself, or when fireworks are present you can leave it on for longer.

Never leave your dog alone while he is wearing a wrap in case he gets caught up. Keep a close eye on him in case you need to make adjustments for comfort or safety, or if he wants it taken off. On very rare occasions some dogs appear to not tolerate body wraps at all. This may be down to an underlying health or pain issue so do consult your vet.

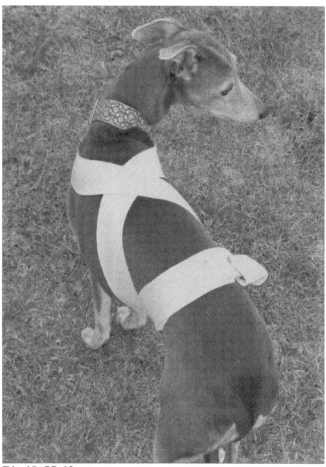

Pic 15: Half wrap *(image courtesy of Toni Shelbourne)*

You can see body wraps being demonstrated online: visit You Tube and search for 'Tellington TTouch for Dogs' and you will find plenty of video clips.

THUNDERSHIRT

In recent years various products have appeared on the market which can be used as an alternative to a body wrap.

The best known of these is probably the Thundershirt, produced by a company which worked alongside Linda Tellington Jones in its development.

The Thundershirt's comfortable, constant contact has a similarly calming effect to a wrap, is easy to put on, and is adjustable to fit different body shapes.

As with using wraps, a Thundershirt should be introduced carefully, breaking the process down into easy stages. It is secured using Velcro straps, and before fitting it, you should make sure that your dog is comfortable with the sound they make.

Extra training and time may be required for dogs with hyper-noise sensitivity, especially if they are reactive to household noises such as frying food, bleeps on electrical equipment and the slamming of doors.

Spend some time over a few sessions introducing the noise to him, but if the sound of the Velcro is just too much for him, it is recommended that you stick with a body wrap or doggie T-shirt instead.

Otherwise, the first step is to allow your dog to inspect it. Putting the Thundershirt on the floor and placing a few really tasty treats on top will encourage him to check it out and help in creating a positive association and overcoming any concerns he may have about it.

Next, unfold it half way and lay it across his back for a few moments, while offering a few more treats if necessary, as he gets used to the feeling.

If he is fine with this, you can then open the Thundershirt up completely and put it on, closing the front fastening but leaving the side panels open. When your dog is happy about this, you can then close the side panels to create a snug fit *(pic 16).*

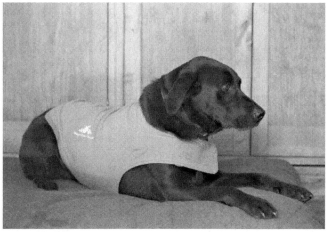

Pic 16: Thundershirt   *(courtesy of Sarah Fisher)*

Again, as with using wraps, keep the initial introductory sessions and periods wearing it short; but once your dog is accustomed to wearing it, it can be left on for as long as required, although you should not leave him in it while unsupervised.

THE CONFIDENCE COURSE

Known as the Confidence Course or playground of higher learning, what at first glance may look like an obstacle course is far from it. As the name suggests, the object of this Tellington TTouch groundwork exercise is to promote confidence rather than to intentionally trip up, confuse or impede your dog. It encourages clear, rational thinking and planning –

things that often go out the window when fear is present – and as your dog makes his way round it can help him to make massive shifts for the better in his thinking and responses. As well as boosting confidence, this exercise is also terrific for developing co-operation, coordination and communication between you.

While groundwork is suggested here as a way of helping your dog to cope with his fear of fireworks, you may find that it can also benefit him in other areas too. Because it improves proprioception it is very useful in teaching agility dogs to move more effortlessly and efficiently, or to help dogs that pull on the leash to find their balance. It can similarly be used for older dogs as a low impact exercise to maintain flexibility and provide mental stimulation. If your dog suffers from motion sickness in the car, very often it can help with travelling issues too.

You can set up a Confidence course outdoors or indoors – working inside can be a way, like having a mini-training session, of giving your dog something else to think about while all the noises are happening outside. You should already have introduced your dog to the idea in advance so that it is something which he is already familiar with.

You do not need lots of expensive equipment, but can easily improvise using objects you either already have to hand or can buy very cheaply. Short lengths of plastic guttering, plastic plumbing pipes, foam pipe lagging or old broom handles make great poles which can be laid out on the ground for your dog to walk over *(pic 17)*.

Slightly raise one or both ends of some poles by crushing an empty drink can in the centre to form a rest for the pole; or scatter them in a random 'pick up sticks' style pile which he has to pick his way through.

Pic 17: Confidence Course *(courtesy of Sarah Fisher)*

Use old bicycle tyres to similarly create mini-mazes to walk through. A short length of scaffold plank can be stepped over or walked along: raise one or both ends by placing a piece of half-profile plastic guttering beneath to create a low raised walkway: use pieces of carpet, rubber bath mats, non-slip plastic and other materials to provide different textures and feels beneath his paws. You could even press the doormat from the front door into service! If you have a foam mattress from a garden lounger it will create a surface that yields slightly as he walks across it, giving yet another different experience: indoors you could use cushions from the sofa or pillows from your bed. Try introducing a slalom, setting out a line of plastic squash bottles weighted by half filling them with water, or empty upturned plastic plant pots, or sports cones which he can weave in and out of. Be inventive and imaginative – as long as the objects you choose are safe, you can create endless variations to keep your dog engaged.

Once you have a few obstacles set up, pop your dog on the leash so you can help to guide him to each one in turn and can encourage him to slow down if he tries to rush. It is best to use a harness rather than attaching the leash to the collar as an inadvertent tug on his neck which raises his head can put him into a state of arousal, which is exactly the opposite effect to the one you are trying to create.

Ask your dog to approach and then slowly move over, through or onto each of the obstacles in turn – it is not a race! If he rushes, he is more likely to become unbalanced and to make mistakes. Moving slowly will encourage him to move with greater deliberation and precision, developing his physical control and self-restraint. Ask him to stop frequently, both in front of and after completing each obstacle, as well as while standing on it so he can collect himself physically, mentally and emotionally. Halting will help make him more aware of his movements, and encourage him to focus his attention on the task in hand and to carefully plan his next move. If you need to give a little signal on the leash to encourage your dog to slow down or stop, remember to gently and slowly allow the tension on it to go slack afterwards, otherwise you will interfere with his balance.

Once he is focussed on the ground work exercises, you can carefully introduce perceived threats such as other dogs or people, or teach self-control around high arousal situations like cyclists and joggers: or in this case, firework noises (see the section on desensitization). With another focus i.e. concentrating on working round the Confidence course the 'threat' can become more tolerable and with the aid of reward-based training and the other TTouch tools, a dog can learn to be comfortable in these highly charged situations. As already mentioned, ground work can help a dog to make massive changes in the way he responds to situations, helping to guide him into making a more measured response instead of flipping into a fear response such as flight: in some cases, noise sensitive dogs will choose to run to their owners for support when they hear a noise, instead of bolting.

You can see the Confidence course being demonstrated online: visit You Tube and search for 'Tellington TTouch for Dogs' and you will find plenty of video clips.

Finally … Help is at Hand!

Many people feel, like we did, that there is no help for your firework phobic pet. We are often led to believe that there is nothing you can do or that drugs are the only option. You may consider your dog's behaviour to be unchangeable, that 'he has always been this way' and therefore will continue to be so. We can tell you that this is not true, help is at hand and fears *can* be overcome. It does however, take time and dedication from you.

Firstly, seek the help of a qualified, reputable professional if you feel you are uncertain about following the suggestions in this book.

Secondly, don't give up, as there is so much that can be done and with the right advice and investment from you, you really can help your dog's fear subside. Although we can't guarantee that the fear will abate entirely, we can predict that you will see changes for the better. If nothing else, following the steps laid out in this book will positively influence the relationship you have with your dog.

FURTHER READING

Acu-Dog: A Guide to Canine Acupressure by Amy Snow & Nancy Zidonis *(Tallgrass Publishing)*

A La Bark Baking by Kris Owen *(Matador)*

All Wrapped up for Pets: Improving function, performance and behaviour with Tellington TTouch Body Wraps by Robyn Hood (available from TTEAM offices – see Contacts & Resources for details

Bach Flower Remedies for Dogs by Martin J Scott and Gael Mariani *(Findhorn Press)*

Canine Behaviour: A Photo Illustrated Handbook by Barbara Handelman *(First Stone)*

Clever Dog! By Gwen Bailey *(Collins)*

Dinner for Dogs by Henrietta Morrison *(Ebury Press)*

Essential Care for Dogs: A Holistic Way of Life by Jackie Drakeford and Mark Elliott MRCVS *(Swan Hill Press)*

Getting in TTouch with Your Dog: A gentle approach to influencing behaviour, health and performance by Linda Tellington-Jones *(Quiller Publishing)*

Harnessing your Dog's Perfection: Helping your dog be the best they can be on leash and in life

with the Tellington TTouch Method by Robyn Hood & Mandy Pretty *(available from TTEAM offices – see Contacts & Resources for contact details)*

Help Your Dog Heal Itself: A-Z guide to using essential oils and herbs for hidden and common problems through the aromatic language of dogs by Caroline Ingraham *(Ingraham Trading Ltd)*

Homeopathic Care for Cats and Dogs by Don Hamilton, DVM *(North Atlantic Books)*

On Talking Terms with Dogs by Turid Rugaas *(First Stone)*

Real Dog Yoga by Jo-Rosie Haffenden *(The Pet Book Publishing Company)*

The Truth about Wolves and Dogs by Toni Shelbourne *(Hubble & Hattie)*

The Holistic Dog: A Complete Guide to Natural Health Care by Holly Mash *(Crowood Press)*

Unlock Your Dog's Potential: How to achieve a calm and happy canine by Sarah Fisher *(David & Charles)*

100 Ways to Train the Perfect Dog by Sarah Fisher and Marie Miller *(David & Charles)*

100 Ways to Solve Your Dog's Problems by Sarah Fisher and Marie Miller *(David & Charles)*

CONTACTS & RESOURCES

The references provided in this section are for informational purposes only and do not constitute endorsement of any sources or products. Readers should be aware that the websites listed in this book may change.

ACUPRESSURE

Tallgrass Animal Acupressure Institute
Details of training courses, workshops and a list of practitioners at:
www.animalacupressure.com
See also Further Reading

ADAPTIL

Available from vets, pet shops and online.
www.adaptil.co.uk

AMERICAN HOLISTIC VETERINARY MEDICAL ASSOCIATION
www.ahvma.org

APPLIED ZOOPHARMACOGNOSY

Case studies, training, and a list of practitioners:
www.ingraham.co.uk
See also Further Reading

BACH FLOWER REMEDIES

www.bachcentre.com
www.bachfloweressences.co.uk
www.bachflowerpets.co.uk
As well as the original Bach remedies there are other companies which produce flower remedies, and have even expanded on the original 38 remedies – for preference look for alcohol-free versions.
See also Further Reading

CAT GRASS
Seeds available from
www.suttons.co.uk
www.mr-fothergills.co.uk

CONFIDENCE COURSE EQUIPMENT
If you would like to buy equipment specially designed for dogs, this may be a useful source:
www.activebalance-vetphysio.co.uk/

DESENSITIZATION CDs
Sounds Scary!
www.soundtherapy4pets.co.uk

CLIX Noises and Sounds
www.companyofanimals.co.uk

DIET
All About Dog Food
www.allaboutdogfood.co.uk
See also Further Reading

ESCAPE PROOF HARNESSES
You may find other 'escape proof' harnesses available if you search online but we recommend that you avoid any which tighten around the dog's body. Alternatively you may be able to find a friendly local saddler who will adapt an existing step-in harness for you.
Houdini Harness from Indi-Dog:
www.indi-dog.co.uk
www.indi-dogusa.com
www.indi-dogcanada.com
Ruffwear:
www.ruffwear.co.uk
and www.ruffwear.com

HERBALISM
British Association of Veterinary Herbalists
www.herbalvets.org.uk

HOMEOPATHY
British Association of Homeopathic Veterinary Surgeons
www.bahvs.com

LOST DOGS
www.doglost.co.uk

Vets get scanning
www.vetsgetscanning.co.uk

MUSIC
Through a Dogs Ear
http://throughadogsear.com

MUTT MUFFS
www.safeandsoundpets.com

PET REMEDY
www.petremedy.co.uk

PHYSIOTHERAPISTS
Association of Chartered Physiotherapists in Animal Therapy
www.acpat.org

McTimoney Chiropractic
www.mctimoneychiropractic.org
www.mctimoney-animal.org.uk

Bowen Technique
www.bowen-technique.co.uk

REAL DOG YOGA
Info and instructor list
www.therealdogyoga.co.uk

SOCIALISATION
Sounds sociable
www.soundtherapy4pets.co.uk

SOUND PROOF KENNELS
The Quiet Kennel
www.prestigepets.co.uk/quiet-kennel

The ZenCrate
www.zendogcrate.com

TELLINGTON TTOUCH
Information, equipment, books, DVDs, links to online
videos, or to find a practitioner:

TTouch Australia
www.listeningtowhispers.com

TTouch Austria
www.tteam.at

Tellington TTouch Canada
5435 Rochdell Road
Vernon, B.C. V1B 3E8
www.tteam-ttouch.ca

TTouch Germany
www.tteam.de

TTouch Ireland
www.ttouchteam-ireland.com

TTouch Italy
www.tteam.it

TTouch Japan
www.ttouch.jp

TTouch Netherlands
www.tteam-ttouch.nl

TTouch New Zealand
www.listeningtowhispers.com

Tellington TTouch South Africa
www.ttouchsa.co.za

TTouch Switzerland
www.tellingtonttouch.ch

Tellington TTouch UK
Tilley Farm
Bath BA2 0AB
Tel: 01761 471182
www.ttouchtteam.co.uk

Tellington TTouch USA
1713 State Road 502
Santa Fe, NM 87506
www.ttouch.com

THUNDERSHIRTS
Available from Tellington TTouch office: see above

TOYS
Kong toys
www.kongcompany.com

Nina Ottosson activity toys and puzzles
www.nina-ottosson.com

Snuffelmats
www.snuffelmat.nl/en_GB

TRAINING & BEHAVIOUR
Association of INTOdogs
www.intodogs.org

Association of Pet Behaviour Councillors
www.apbc.com

Association of Pet Dog Trainers
www.apdt.co.uk

Association of Pet Dog Trainers (US)
www.apdt.com

International Companion Animal Network
http://companionanimal.network/

TREATS
Lily's Kitchen Organic Bedtime Biscuits
www.lilyskitchen.co.uk

Pooch & Mutt Calm and Relaxed Dog Treats
www.poochandmutt.com

WHITE NOISE MACHINES
Lectrofan
www.soundofsleep.com

NOTES

EARLY NEUTERING
If you suspect your dog is suffering from the effects of early neutering this video by Dr Karen Becker provides more information:
http://products.mercola.com/healthypets/canine-hormone-support

HERBAL PREPARATIONS
Valerian: **www.petnutritioninfo.com/valerian-root-benefits.html**
Hops: **www.petpoisonhelpline.com/poison/hops**

MEDICATION
Various medications are available from your vet that may be helpful, and you should discuss with him the pro's and cons involved and suitability for your dog. Some are not suitable for long term use and many have a long list of side effects. The NOAH Compendium of Animal Medicines is a useful online resource which will enable you to find out more about known contra-indications and side effects of the various products available, so that in combination with your vet's guidance, you can make an informed decision about their use. Search by either product name or active ingredient at:
www.noahcompendium.co.uk

MUSIC
Research studies on the effects of music on dogs:
Wells, D. L., et al. "The Influence of Auditory Stimulation on the Behaviour of Dogs Housed in a Rescue Shelter." *Animal Welfare 11 (2002): 385-393*

Wagner, S., et al. *BioAcoustic Research & Development Canine Research Summary* (2004)

You can read more about the effects of bioacoustics music and listen to samples on the website at Through a Dog's Ear:
http://throughadogsear.com

ABOUT THE AUTHORS

TONI SHELBOURNE
Animal Behaviourist, Tellington TTouch Practitioner, Real Dog Yoga Instructor & Author

Toni has worked with domesticated and wild canids since 1989. After a long and successful career with the Guide Dogs for the Blind Association, she started her own business as a Tellington TTouch Companion Animal Practitioner. She is now one of the highest qualified Practitioners in the UK. In 2001 her skills in TTouch took Toni to the UK Wolf Conservation Trust where she meet a pack of socialised wolves. She went on to work with them for over a decade as a Senior Wolf Handler and Education Officer for the organisation. In more recent years, Toni has gone on to become a Real Dog Yoga Instructor, and updated her qualifications in behaviour with the International School of Psychology and Behaviour, for which she is also an affiliate. She is now a full member of The Association of INTO Dogs as a certified canine behaviourist and the International Companion Animal Network as a certified Animal Behaviourist. She teaches all over the UK and abroad, gives webinars, works with clients' one to one, and writes. Toni lives in Oxfordshire, England with her husband and their dog MrP.

Email:
ttouch1@btconnect.com
Website:
www.tonishelbourne.co.uk
Facebook:
The Truth about Wolves & Dogs
Twitter:
@tonishelbourne

KAREN BUSH

Karen is a qualified riding teacher and since leaving school has combined working with horses with writing about them and about her other great love, dogs. She has written hundreds of features for leading national publications including Horse & Rider, Your Horse, Pony, Horse & Pony, Horse, and Your Dog and over twenty books including the best-selling 'The Dog Expert'. Karen currently shares her home with two rescue whippets.

Websites:
www.karenbush.jimdo.com
www.dogfriendlygardening.jimdo.com
Blog:
www.dogfriendlygardening.blogspot.co.uk
Facebook:
Dog friendly gardening

INDEX

Toni and Karen can be contacted at:

Website:
www.tonishelbourneandkarenbush.jimdo.com

and on Facebook at
Ebooks by Toni Shelbourne and Karen Bush

Printed in Great
Britain
by Amazon